THE HEDGE

Todd Johnson
and the Story of Pomifera® Oil

TODD JOHNSON
and ROBERT JOSEPH AHOLA

For Susan, Emily, Leah,
Dad, Mom and Uncle Don

TABLE OF CONTENTS

AUTHOR'S NOTE

There is no perfect time to write a book. What I have learned in the process of putting this together is that stories that need to be told take on a life of their own. They are like seeds of truth that, once planted, cannot be denied the right to flourish. They have to be sewn and watered and given room to grow—finally revealing the truth of what they are.

That is what the story of Pomifera® has been for me. In its way this strange natural phenomenon has always been a fringe player in my life. The trees were everywhere in southern Iowa where I grew up. In fact *Maclura Pomifera* (the Latin designation) are prolific in about 37 of the 48 contiguous United States. And up until recently, it was the tree that was believed useful and very much in demand while its strange "ugly duckling" fruit was regarded as little more than a curious kind of seasonal outgrowth and something of nuisance at that.*

---

* In fact, the Comanche and other Native American warriors used wood from the Maclura Pomifera tree to carve out what were regarded as the finest bows for hunting and warfare ever found among the indigenous tribes of North America.

Hedgeballs, hedge apples, horse apples, Osage oranges, "monkey balls," *bois d'arc,* bodark, bodock—all these names and more were attributed to the sticky, crusty, pockmarked green fruit that adorned its branches only to fall to the ground somehow castoff by Nature, unused, undesirable and (seemingly) unacceptable. But wait a minute!

I have a science background, a PhD in Chemistry. And I'm not telling you this to impress you (maybe a little bit), as much I am willing to share with you the one thing we learn in every laboratory in the world: Virtually nothing in Nature goes to waste. There does seem to be a purpose for all things under Heaven. And as Aristotle once observed: "Nature abhors a vacuum."

This certainly applies to the Osage Orange, aka *Pomifera®*.

I admit to a bias here. I grew up surrounded by arbors and woods filled with these strange castoffs. And Native American lore about their medicinal uses were more than supported by my dear departed, larger-than-life, self-made millionaire great uncle Don Prevo who insisted until the day he died that, "There's something 'magical' in those hedge balls."

Uncle Don was a man with impeccable instincts. And his insistence that these little rogue green clumps cluttering the groves of Iowa contained one of life's great secrets stuck to me all through the course of my career in science. From legends of its uses to treat everything from eye infections to skin cancer and uterine complications in women, I held onto the healthy curiosity that any committed scientist must embrace—that there is some strain of truth in every legend, and that everything in this garden of Nature deserves a second look.

So, in a way, for years my career path and Pomifera's ran along parallel lines—finding touching points at various times— but always on the periphery of my awareness. It stayed with me through some of the major sci- ence and technology companies in the world, through a dozen plus patents and a host of science and compliance realities that only come when one learns to navigate that narrow corridor between the laboratory and the boardroom, and how to "develop the busi- ness side of science."

POMIFERA*oil*™
WHERE FOLKLORE MEETS BEAUTY™

Finally there came that point of critical mass when enough "hedge apples" crossed my path to bring me to make that final intersection— that leap of faith to dare and uncover the treasure locked inside.

The rest that followed is a miracle of discovery that has brought life-changing experiences to thousands of people, and set free a "One Drop Wonder™" whose mysteries have only begun to be explored. Along the way it has generated a cottage industry that is about to blow up along with a network market- ing mega-movement beyond all our expectations.

Inspired by Pomifera's phenomenal, life-changing potentials, I knew I had to share all the remarkable experiences that have already unfolded on this journey. It has turned out to be a once- in-a-lifetime undertaking, and I needed a fellow traveler to help frame it with the kind of intelligent passion that it deserved.

I'm a fairly decent writer. And my PhD thesis in Chemistry demanded that kind of discipline to compile and create a book to summarize my five plus years of research. But this saga involving the discovery and development of Pomifera® was already starting to unfold like an action-adventure novel. And, given my intense schedule and 60 hour a week workload, I knew it would take me five years at least to put together the kind of story this 25-year mosaic would create.

So I decided I would need a co-conspirator. And in my searches I came across Malibu, California based author and playwright Robert Joseph Ahola.

Robert has authored and co-authored at least 25 books covering everything from visionary fiction to a *Complete Wellness Guidebook*. His range of interests have included pop-psychology, biographies of famous people and such science encyclopedias as *The Silent Healer* and *Creatures in Our Care* (a coffee table pictorial on holistic animal care). He also built quite a resumé as an advertising and marketing Creative Director. Combine that with an obvious bent toward science writing and research, and Robert was a man I felt whose abilities complemented my own.

Besides, he answered every query I sent his way with a sense of both comfort and comprehension I didn't find in anyone else. Robert tends to write non-fiction with a novelist's sense of intrigue and a satirist's nose for comedy. So he convinced me at least that this would be venture worth undertaking. A series of productive conversations convinced us both that this was story that could pay homage to tradition while exploring a special vision for the future.

What's more, we both felt that this was something of a treasure hunt, and that it needed to be told in a way that uncovered the mystery while it helped everyone reading this learn more about how we got there.

Robert had an idea about how to do it that was unique, organic and non-linear. And he'll tell you how we're going to go about it, so I'll pass you along to him.

After that, I'll see the rest of you inside the book... ☺

~ Todd Johnson

INTRODUCTION

ynchronicity. It is a term coined by psychoanalyst Garl Gustav Jung to describe, "a divinely inspired occurrence disguised as a coincidence." From my point of view, an occasion of synchronicity requires a few elements to make it happen. First, it contains something in the universe that insists upon being born to human consciousness. Second, it has to come into contact with some genius at the physical level to bring it to maturity. Third, it requires someone with a sense of determination to bring it all the way to life. It needs an initiator, a forerunner, and an advocate.

If one word would describe Todd Johnson it would be "resolution." Fortunately, as a professional writer—and a self-confessed "word drunk"—I'm not limited to one description. Todd is upon first impression what I call *a high life force human being.* He knows his purpose. And it was clear to me upon our first conversation that he is gifted with a sense of vision that few people possess.

Todd sees things clearly. He has a scientist's ability to question, analyze and develop a concept, and an entrepreneur's

instincts for what really works and how to translate that working
model into a success. He also possesses a sense of enthusiasm that
is downright contagious. Because when he believes in something,
he is also determined to share that belief.

That's what had me rooting for him going into our series of
"getting to know you" discussions, a cordial chain of interactions
that took place in early 2017.

"I'm not quite sure how this is going to come about," he told
me. "But I'm sure it's a story that needs to be told."

The story he was most intent upon telling was his discovery
of Pomifera® Oil, and the twists and turns that led him to this
point on his life's path.

I don't always take on every assignment or project set in front
of me. If it's not something I have initiated on my own—if I'm
going to collaborate on a book or film—I want to believe that it
will be a subject worth talking about.

In this case, I was a sympathetic ear, because I am passion-
ately driven to support three things: health & wellness, the environment and making this world a better place. So here was a
subject set before me—Pomifera®—that actually promised to be
a commitment to all three.

I like to think I have a Renaissance command of many subjects, and my writing in the field of science and health technology has been extensive.

So I immediately saw that the subject Todd was promoting—his discovery and development of this miraculous oil that
came out of something called hedge apples—had tremendous
potential.

Nature's pharmacy is prodigious. There are over 390,000
plant species on planet Earth and the vast majority of them are

useful for something. The *Pharmacopoeias* of every healer from Hippocrates to Deepak Chopra are replete with plant, floral and herbal remedies for virtually every condition known to humankind. And what most people don't realize is that many if not most prescription pharmaceuticals and OTC drugs have a botanical base.

Todd Johnson knew that. And he knew, as we both did, that all progress in his field occurred because some intrepid scientist, some adventurer, dared to boldly go "where no one has gone before."

That was Todd all over. My series of conversations with him over several months revealed that in no small measure. While we were trying to rearrange our busy schedules, I came to see in Todd Johnson a rare combination of a human being—one who combined an athlete's swagger with a lab nerd's gift for intellectual sagacity and meticulous research, managing all the while to toss in a savvy businessman's foresight about how to get things to market.

Of course, he didn't get there overnight. And the tale of how he did, and how one man managed to navigate the science labs and board rooms of some of the most sophisticated science and technology companies in the world to discover, refine, create and bring to market what has come to be known as the "One Drop Wonder™" makes for an episodic adventure all its own.

That is the one I'm hoping to help Todd Johnson bring to you now. It is not only an action-adventure/spy-saga, it is also a success story, a "rags to riches" classic, and something of a marketing primer. And it is one we're delighted to bring to you on the next 200 plus pages.

For those who know Todd, it should come as no surprise to find out that this book is going to be put together in a way that is completely different from most biographies or "memoirs" you have read. Almost from the beginning of our relationship, Todd's integrity inserted itself into the equation, in a very good way.

In Todd Johnson's words: "I don't like acting as if I've written something if I haven't done it 100%."

So it was my suggestion that, "You shouldn't. Let's have a series of conversations—interviews if you will. That way we can cover all the subjects you need to. We can capture everything you need to say and recount your many adventures in a way that is candid, kinetic and very much in your own voice."

As it is one of his great skills to acknowledge a good idea, whatever the source, Todd immediately caught the energy of the concept I proposed and embraced it.

So with Todd's consent, his direction and his whole-hearted participation, we will be creating a non-linear, highly energetic, living document. And because it is both alive and in a state of perpetual motion, it will be something you can read, jump into at any point, and come away feeling you've spent some time in a book, a story, a life and a house where all the doors and windows remain open.

It is also an experience from which, we believe, you will extract considerable knowledge, some new ways to see your world and a *sense of motivation* to go out and accomplish great things.

We also hope you'll enjoy yourself in the process…

~ Robert Joseph Ahola

CHAPTER 1

A NEW DYNAMIC

An unexamined life is not worth living
~ Aristotle

Todd Johnson has an athlete's way of negotiating a room—whether it's a laboratory, a marketing meeting or on stage with a microphone in front of a crowd of thousands of LimeLight Beauty Guides. With a physical prowess cultivated on the baseball diamonds and football fields of the Midwest, he has a mesomorphic sense of awareness that instills confidence in just about everything he does. He has an instinct about how to use media to put things in a favorable light. Todd is directive without being manipulative. And he engages everything he does with a boundless sense of joy that is downright contagious.

Part of that *joy de vivre* carries with it the contagion of success. Todd and his Pomifera® Oil are currently on a roll. Todd is a winner. From what I can see, he always has been. (But he is about to disabuse me of that fact, insisting with a glint in his eye that, "For a long time I really didn't have my act together.")

That was ancient history, as you soon will see. So, for now, let us focus on the moment. And for the moment, I'm going into my first interview with Todd Johnson, PhD, CEO of Osage Healthcare, Inc. creator of the juggernaut Pomifera®. It will be the flagship conversation of many that will comprise this book, not only with Todd but also with several key people in his life—his family, his co-workers, some mentors and many who have been influenced by the man and his mission.

Above all else we're going to find out in this chapter what makes this man and his story so extraordinary. And we are giving this book the title of *THE HEDGE.* It's an obvious play on words that I'm sure I won't have to go very far to explain. There is an "Edge" to this book of course, and that goes to the man himself.

To no one's surprise, Todd Johnson is not a "coat and tie" executive. He works in shirtsleeves (usually rolled up) or a sweatshirt or sweater…and occasionally some "camo" fatigues when he's in the field. At all times, he appears ready to dive in and get his hands dirty. In fact, he does so on occasion. In fact he insists that others do as well. In truth, Todd has built this business from the ground up—with a great deal of sweat equity—and has done everything from *Genesis* to this moment, from piling the hedge apples that come into his facilities by the truckload, to research and refining in the labs, to designing the original harvesting machines, to making personal appearances at LimeLight Palooza.

Going in, I tease Todd that he has now *ex-officio* become the George Washington Carver of Pomifera®.* He laughs out-

---

* Making no assumptions here, the reference I made to George Washington Carver is that he is the botanist and inventor who researched and developed a certain food called the Peanut. Originally considered a junk crop only fed to pigs, peanuts were initially thought to be unfit for human consumption. Dr. Carver used his tenure at Tuskegee Institute to research, develop and cultivate peanuts and sweet potatoes as replacement crops to be rotated with cotton (a notorious ravager of farmlands). As a result his 44 pamphlets featuring over 114 recipes for peanuts, including something called Peanut Butter, ended in revolutionizing modern consumer habits for more than a century. Peanut products have since fed tens of millions of people on seven continents, and have subsequently become a $4.5 billion industry ($2.2 billion in peanut butter alone) with over 43 million tons of peanuts produced every year.

loud at the thought of it. But in fact it's the absolute truth. For every great discovery on earth, there is that driving force—that man or men or women who bring that movement about. Todd Johnson is that guy. Pomifera® is that story. And this is where it begins.

(As a note: In my interviews with Todd I will refer to myself as RJA, and Todd Johnson will [at all times] be Todd.) One thing I immediately notice about Todd is the fact that he is animated.

Even when he's sitting still he is in a constant state of perpetual motion. When he isn't teaching, he is learning. Every moment seems to be an opportunity for him, and that tends to make a man anything but dull.

RJA: *So here we are in your world, and it all still seems so new. From what I've learned you've gone from a cold start about three years ago to the exponential growth you enjoy today. And you seem to take it all in stride. First of all, I'm surprised—given your rapidly growing sphere of influence—that your operation isn't physically larger. Second, you spend so much time here, and yet you actually seem to be enjoying every moment of it.*

Todd: You're right. I do spend great deal of time doing this. But if I've learned anything over the years it is that you have to have an absolute passion for what you're doing. Because life is going to be a very long drudge if you don't. You asked about the size of our operation here at Pomifera. The staff is small but extremely efficient and very well trained. In fact, everyone here is trained to do everyone else's job. So in the case of an emergency or places where we need some extra help they can slot in at a moment's notice.

RJA: *Even at your job?*

Todd: Oh, absolutely! I make certain of that. My wife Susan could take over right now if anything were to happen to me, and make it work beautifully. (At least for a time.) One of the Rules of The Road for me has always been, "If you make yourself irreplaceable then you're doomed to be stuck in that place." I also believe that, if you're going to really grow to your fullest potential, you always hire the best people and let them do what they do best. You always build your team with people who are smarter than you are. In fact, I'm happy to be the dumbest guy in the room.

RJA: *...Which, from what I can see, you never are. I mean here you are with a PhD in Chemistry, a former science and marketing rockstar with international Chem-Agra conglomerates like Monsanto, a major factor in half a dozen science, chemical and marketing "players" in the field of APIs (Active Pharmaceutical Ingredients) and holder of about 20 patents.*

Todd: Actually it's somewhere around 12 patents – give or take a couple. But I don't want to make more of them than they really are. So that's something we can cover later.

RJA: *Still, it does underscore the fact that you bring a ton of credentials and about 25 years of intense experience to whatever you do. Not too many people can boast that kind of "cred."*

Todd: Well, it all looks good on your CV or resumé. But there's a lot more to it than that. One thing I picked up on immediately while I was at Monsanto was that just about everyone there was my equal. Virtually everyone there had academic pedigrees and were loaded up with credentials. The difference was finding the right people and cultivating the core group to get you to the next level. That meant you couldn't allow yourself to be threatened by people. You had to be willing to clone yourself when you had to do so.

RJA: *Is that one of Todd Johnson's Rules Of The Road (ROTR)?*

Todd: It certainly dovetails into one of them.

RJA: *I notice in our conversations that you've actually got about 3 sets of Rules Of The Road: one for personal behavior, one for professional strategy, and one for science and business analysis. So I guess this goes to your personal set.*

Todd: Well, it's really a crossover. Most things are. But I don't want to confuse my *Rules Of The Road* with my personal *Code of Ethics,* because they apply in slightly different ways. Essentially my Rules Of The Road go something like this: *First, most people want clear direction.* They want to know where they stand and what you expect of them. They want to be able to rely on you to be true to your word and that you expect the same of them. That way there's a shared sense of responsibility and a clear set of objectives going forward.

Next, they want to work in a non-hostile environment. Harmony and trust are very important ingredients in any relationship—business or personal—and you have to bring your integrity into every relationship in everything you do. That requires that you remain objective at all times. Don't get personal, and don't take things personally. And whatever you do, never lose your cool. Nothing kills your credibility more quickly than being an emotional hip-shooter.

Third, people want good general communication and teamwork. They want to be able to trust that team. They want to be able to bring both their problems and their solutions to you without concern for outcome. A good leader will recognize that, acknowledge the difference and instill in his or her team that you never assess blame or pass the buck. ***People function best in an environment where retribution is never a response to taking risk.***

RJA: *Those are a lot of absolutes. Aren't we taught never to say "never?"*

Todd: And aren't these the exceptions that prove the rule? I personally can't think of a single time when anyone assessed blame or made excuses or looked for scapegoats when it actually made something better. In fact it blocks the way to one of my most important Rules Of The Road: *Always bring an ability to accept good ideas* no matter where they come from. Be constantly driven to result.

We've all heard tales about executives or political leaders or scientists who can't recognize a good idea unless it is their own. You never want to be that guy. Because that is the end of all progress. Great leaders empower others. They make them feel valuable. I've had that done for me along my journey. And I always want to do that for others. That's what builds a team. That's what makes you stronger and gives you that synergy all great teams, groups or companies have. And that brings us full circle to my final ROTR: *Always build your team with people who are smarter than you are.* When you surround yourself, your group and your company with a team of really quality people—bright people, good people, positive people—you're only going to get better.

It's been apparent to me from the beginning that we never really take this journey alone. We get where we are by recognizing the value of the human dynamic and the kind of synergy we can create with people who actually make us better by our relationships with them.

RJA: *That's the Law of Attraction, in fact. That's what Napoleon Hill described as "Mastermind" groups.*** *So do you feel as if you've always had that in every set of circumstances?*

Todd: I don't think anyone bats a thousand. But if you're going to succeed and be at your best you have to have the best around you—the best and brightest people, the best attitudes and the most consistently shared objectives. If I've always been blessed with anything it is with those things above all others. For the most part, I've had phenomenal exchanges and relationships with my teachers and coaches in school, and so many mentors and partners in business. And it certainly begins and ends with my own family—from my flawed but loving father to my incredible wife Susan and my daughters Emily and Leah. I'm a very lucky man.

RJA: *I've already gotten a good look at how devoted you are to your family, and they to you. But your Rules Of The Road seem geared*

**Napoleon Hill is the author of *Think and Grow Rich*. With more than 100 million copies in circulation, it is the bestselling personal success manual of all time.

a little more toward business. Do you have some personal inserts as well? I mean I'm sort of asking a rhetorical question, because I already know a couple— like "Be Honest in all things. Be clear about who you are and what you want..."

Todd: We'll you could more or less say they are rules my father taught me. But the rest more or less go as follows: "Always go to result. Always be success oriented. Be objective in all things. Never pass the buck (I covered that earlier). Don't lose your cool. (Stay calm and focused at all times.) And Always bring a high level of integrity in whatever you do."

That means being willing to take responsibility for things— whether it's a project, a relationship, or a company like this. Don't be afraid to put yourself on the line.

RJA: *Those are some pretty high standards.*

Todd: Yeah. Well, just off the top of my head, I can't think of anyone making much of their life by having low standards.

RJA: *Amen to that! And by now, I certainly know a lot about what you are. But what I'd like to do now is discuss who you are. Who is Todd Johnson after all, and why does he want to do this book? I know it's to tell the story of Pomifera and sync it into the life of Todd Johnson along the way. But why are you doing this really? One of your Rules Of The Road is to "state your objectives clearly." So what are they? Why is it that you want to do this book and why is it important that you do so?*

Todd. Actually there are several reasons, but they really distill down to about three. First, I think it's time to tell the story of

Pomifera® Oil. It's a genuine revelation. And it's quite a break-through to be able to share this magnificent discovery with others. It can actually change lives. (It already has.) I truly believe we're just scratching the surface where this incredible natural vegan oil is concerned.

I also know in my heart that there truly are no accidents. My involvement with this wonderful thing called Pomifera Oil came at a point of perfect convergence. It may have seemed like I just stumbled upon it, but it had been implanted in my conscious-ness since I was a young boy. That story needs to be told.

I also realized that my whole career—my entire life's path to this point if you will—has been guided to this phenomenal chain of findings. It took my science background to be able to breakdown and analyze the chemical composition of this natural wonder. And there is no question that unless I was able to take an Eastern medicine approach to the discovery itself, I never could have come to the solid science based results I achieved. So it's really a miracle of discovery; and a leap of faith.

RJA: *And it's obviously something you are obviously passionate about sharing. But it's more about just telling that story. It also goes a long way into telling yours—which is certainly a success story.*

Todd: It's that too. And I'm both humbled and grateful to share it. I mean, here I am, a poor kid from the trailer courts of south-ern Iowa, and somehow I'm able to get a PhD in Chemistry from a major Big Ten University, go into a major Fortune 500 company like Monsanto as a research chemist, learn how to take rigorous science and translate it into a solid set of business applications.

RJA: *Let me interrupt you right there. Because that makes you the rarest of the rare. It almost never happens that a "science-nerd" becomes a marketing mogul.*

Todd: Yes and no. Because Monsanto was the perfect training ground for just that concept. At Monsanto it was almost a job requirement that you learn how to take rigorous science and bring it into the boardroom. You have to cross-pollinate science discoveries and refine them into business applications that work. Otherwise you're stuck in one place forever. And one thing I have never done is get stuck. In fact I made so many changes in my life—and so many career moves in a short time—that to an outsider it might look absolutely frivolous.

RJA: *But it wasn't. Every one of your career moves—from what I can see—were up the ladder. You were in demand everywhere you went. Almost like a star in the NFL or NBA.*

Todd: I wish I had their money. But it was quite a string of events. And one worth telling, I think. And I think I may have gotten a little off the track, because my point here about my life and career this far is that I want to show others how it's done; because if I can do it, anyone can do it.

RJA: *Anyone? That's a pretty broad-sweeping claim. Do you really think anyone can do this?*

Todd: Oh absolutely. Anyone can do it, if they apply certain principles. Of course, they won't do exactly what I did by following my recommendations. Everyone has her or his own path. It's different for everyone. That's for sure.

But if my story can motivate others to take that leap of faith and pursue their dream, then this book has served its purpose. I want to inspire the reader who has the sense that they can compete way above their socioeconomic level. I seriously want to empower the person "from the wrong side of the tracks" to take risks. I know they are filled with trepidation and need that "example" to look towards as they reach for the unreachable.

RJA: *But you have some special qualities.*

Todd: I think everyone does. They just have to know how to cultivate them. And it really helps when you have mentors and partners and significant others in your life to help to define who you are and what your path becomes. These are the people who inspire you, advise you, guide you and support you all along the way. We all have them. I have really been blessed to have so many.

RJA: *You mentioned your father... Doy, is it? And you mentioned your wife Susan as special influences in your life.*

Todd: My father, though he struggled personally at times, always inspired my brother Mike and me to believe that there wasn't anything we couldn't accomplish. He taught us to be fearless and to believe in ourselves. That faith always gave me the grit I needed in some tough situations. As far as Susan is concerned, she is the most remarkable woman I've ever known. She has always pulled me back to center. And I couldn't have possibly gotten this far without her. There have been many others, and I'm grateful to all of them.

RJA: *This seems almost too good to be true. Has it been that easy?*

Todd: Define easy. There are always hurdles along the way. I don't think any pathway to success is a straight upward curve. Not in the real world.

RJA: *Ralph Waldo Emerson once said: "Whatever course you decide upon, there is always someone to tell you that you are wrong. There are always difficulties arising that will tempt you to believe your critics were right." Did you ever confront that?*

Todd: Oh, sure I have. I mean, if you haven't you're not really trying. I recognize that quote from Emerson, by the way. He also finished by saying (I believe): "To map out a course of action and follow it requires courage." So he paid it off with a win. And that's what I absolutely believe in.

RJA: *Are you courageous?*

Todd: I hope so. I like to think so. I will tell you one thing: I am driven…and determined. And I don't take no for an answer. Once I decide go for something I'm full bore until I get it accomplished.

RJA: *Sounds like you never fail. Or at least not very often…*

Todd: Oh heavens no! If you have any kind of a career in science and research, you learn that failure is a part of the process. It's not only a part of the process, it's essential to the process. You have to make dozens of mistakes before you come up with the right solution. Failure is the teacher. That is what gives you the chance to stop, reboot and recalibrate your objectives. Failure is that essential step up on the ladder to success.

RJA: *Some people I've interviewed refer to you as a "genius." Either that or "The smartest man I've ever met." Do you own up to that?*

Todd: I hear that from time to time. And I've kind of gotten used to it, I suppose. I don't think anything I'm doing is genius, but it is 150% on the passion scale. I think passion has a kind of genius of its own. And it's the old Thomas Edison maxim: "Genius is 10% inspiration and 90% perspiration." This whole journey has been one of collaboration. So maybe collectively there is some genius in all this.

RJA: *You mentioned three major reasons for doing this book. What is the third?*

Todd: My main reason for doing this is to tell a story that's never been told: *The Story of Pomifera® Oil.* It may be one of Nature's true miracles and, at this point, no one knows much of anything about it. So, above else, I want to shed some light on that... because it can potentially help tens of thousands of people, maybe even millions.

At this point, we have such a terrific relationship with a company called LimeLight by Alcone. It's a company that is a leader in Direct Sales of high quality, natural skincare and cosmetics. They're our partners on this very important journey into the future. And they have a virtual army of passionate Beauty Guides (aka distributors) who are true believers in what we have. So we want to provide them with a story they can share.

Here we have a product that has been brought into being by the best possible evolutionary process—of science and Nature—and it's changing lives. We have so much physical evidence: before and after photos of women who have used the product with extraordinary results.

We make no medical claims for the product. But we are constantly getting feedback from people who have used it to help conditions like skin allergies, eczema and even psoriasis. And—I know these testimonies are all anecdotal but—people are blown away by the results.

So we are just touching the tip of the iceberg.

RJA: *And the iceberg is the rest of the story. So, it's about you and Pomifera Oil and how all of this came into being.*

Todd: All that and so much more.

RJA: *And that is where we pick up next...*

Note: One aspect of Todd Johnson that constantly catches my attention is the fact that he has a kind of carryover passion. It is an aura that follows him around even after a conversation. There is clearly more he wants to tell and will do so at a moment's notice. That makes him an engaging interview—one that is both credible and compelling all at the very same time.

In that regard it provides a narrative that is as alive in the moment as it is confident in its purpose. At this point, I am wondering if we can sustain the energy throughout this journey. So I'm full of questions, but certain in the anticipation that for everything I ask Todd Johnson will have a ready answer.

Todd advised me in the beginning of this relationship that he never takes on anything unless he's absolutely convinced it's the right thing to do. That makes him a rarity—one that in my long career as an author I have only encountered once or twice before.

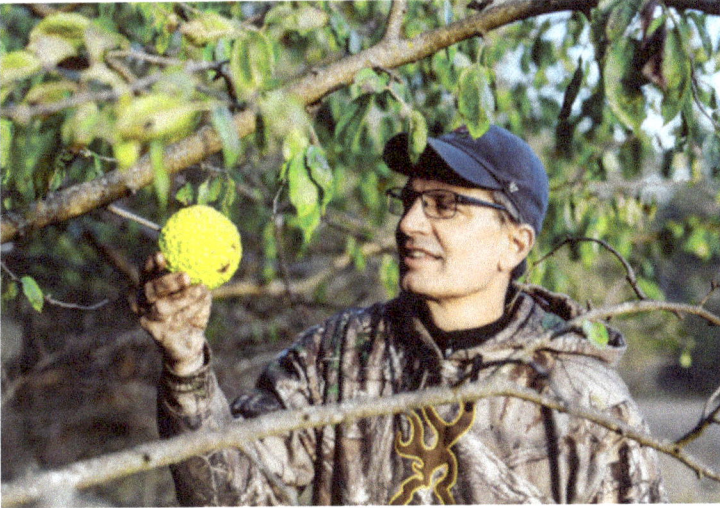

"I think it's time to tell the story of Pomifera® Oil…I truly believe we're just scratching the surface where this incredible natural vegan oil is concerned. I also know in my heart that there truly are no accidents."

~ Todd Johnson

CHAPTER 2

NO LIMITS: FROM A SMALL TOWN TO THE GREAT GAME

"At the age of six I wanted to be a cook.
At seven I wanted to be Napoleon.
My ambition has been growing steadily ever since."

Salvador Dali

By the look of it, Bloomfield, Iowa is everyone's ideal of a small Midwestern town. In the southeastern part of the state near the conjunction of the Missouri and Illinois borders, it is one of those classic boroughs where "everybody knows your name."

An almost quintessential heartland community, Bloomfield has an historical courthouse and a small city square that look picture postcard perfect in the snow. In fact the entire town looks as if it were etched into the Iowa countryside with the careful intention of not disrupting the flow of Nature. Its homes and streets seem to embrace the trees and nearby waterways rather than force them into submission. There is in that symmetry a respect for all things that is missing from every big city in the world. It's not bucolic in the classical sense. But it's not too shabby either. It's just a part of Americana that I hope will never go away.

For that reason and so many more, it is difficult to imagine anyone coming from the wrong side of the tracks in a town this small. And yet Todd Johnson more than occasionally implies that he does.

In a way, it seems pretty hard to find the "tracks" in Bloomfield. According to US census figures it has had the same population, give or take a couple of dozen inhabitants, since the 1970s (about 2,625 in 2010). So it's neither a dying town nor a flourishing hot new market. It is one of those reassuring staples in the American heartland—a rural farm community with its own sense of values and a timeless regard for both civility and tradition. Pulitzer Prize winning author Harper Lee *(To Kill A Mockingbird)*, once famously noted: "In a small town, there are just one kind of folks. Folks!"

For me it was always a salute to the "normal core" of this nation. That's the one that still holds traditional values, treats everyone as equals and offers a respect and trust that—once earned—is there to embrace as something that gives meaning to one's life.

I get from Todd Johnson that he jokes a bit about his "cornfed Midwest upbringing," but I cannot help but notice that, when he brings it up, there is a glint in his eye when he does so.

Todd was born—Todd Jeffrey Johnson—in 1964, the eldest of three children, and son of Doy Edward Johnson and Mary Ellen (Sickle) Johnson—self-confessedly "of humble origins," but with a profound emotional energy and competitive Alphamale edge that was both genetic and environmentally reinforced (something I've concluded but something that he might challenge in equal measure to this day).

On this day, I decided to challenge his self-deprecations and get to the roots… of his roots.

RJA: *So you have mentioned more than once that you want to tell your story by revealing that you've come from the "trailer parks of southern Iowa to become a PhD and something of a business Mogul." Is this kind of an Abraham Lincoln log cabin analogy?*

Todd: I wouldn't say it quite like that. But in a way, yes! This is that kind of rags to riches success story.

RJA: *Was it really always that much "rags?" This is America after all.*

Todd: I'm not trying to oversell it because back in the 1970s when I was growing up, we didn't have any of the access to the social tech toys we have now—the iPhones, the iPads the iMacs, the flat screen TVs—so life was simpler then. Back then, we had to use our imaginations and become inventive in what we did with our spare time. But there were those occasions when I remember that we were living from meal to meal, and just basically making ends meet.

RJA: *OK. So you had a family of five. Four in the beginning because I believe your sister Vicki Lynn was born much later. So you were the first-born, and then came your brother Mike who is a couple of years younger.*

Todd: Right. And I need to emphasize that we never took welfare or anything. So it was never that dire. But we struggled. My father always worked, but we often had what they now call "cash flow" issues.

If I could describe the first few years of my life in Bloomfield it would be to say they were "irregular." My father was a talented man but, through no fault of his own, somewhat undereducated. He had all kinds of skills. And I suppose you would call them blue-collar. But I've always thought people who label others as "blue collar" have never bothered to get their hands dirty. And there is a certain kind of dignity in good hard physical labor. Every farmer in Iowa will tell you that.

In my dad's case, he tried to be entrepreneurial but wasn't the best money manager. For a while he had a successful contract painting company and made $30,000 in one year (which was a lot of money back in the late 1960s). But that was about the same time we got our family Camaro repossessed. So you might say we were always living on the edge.

RJA: *And yet you always speak of your father with an unmistakable sense of love and fondness.*

Todd: Oh absolutely! What we may have lacked in worldly wealth, we made up for in love and regard for one another. Don't get me wrong. Dad was old school. He was a strict disciplinarian. He made sure Mike and I always minded our manners, always stood when adults came into the room, always held doors for women, always said "please and thank you," at the appropriate times, and always observed every kind of social amenity. But he was so much more than that as a dad.

RJA: *In what ways? I'm sure there are more than one.*

Todd: He taught us how to dream. Despite what I would describe as a Pandora's Box of challenges that faced him early in his life, he never lost that ability to have big dreams and encourage us to do the same. And I don't mean that he was delusional. His ambitions always had a practical core, and he instilled in both Mike and me the fact that there was nothing we couldn't accomplish if we set our minds to doing it.

"There are no limits to what you can be," he used to tell me so many times. "You can achieve anything. And there will be those times when you will fail. But there's no reason to fear failure as long as you're doing your best. As long as you keep your integrity, you will ultimately succeed."

RJA: *That's almost a contradiction, isn't it? Here was a man who struggled much of his life and who, at times, had trouble providing for his own family. And yet he sets you up with that kind of confidence to get through life.*

Todd: I guess you'd have to know my dad. He was the archetype for saying, "Do as I say, not as I do!" And it was very endearing in a way. Anytime we had a disappointment or a setback when we were kids, he was there to pick us back up and get us back in the game. He instilled in me at least the will to never give up.

RJA: *Don't you think you had a little of that already?*

Todd: I'm sure I did. It is part of my nature. But you know as well as I that this kind of initiative can be stunted, especially without the proper reinforcement. And Doy Edward Johnson was always there for us. Oddly enough, what I didn't know at the time but learned much later on, was that my dad was treated horribly by his own father.

Discouraged, ridiculed, made to feel small—my dad suffered tremendously at the hands of a very strict overseer of a dad. And he carried those scars of self-doubt with him all his life. To add insult to injury, he was even christened with a girl's name, Doy, because his mother and father, at that point in their parenthood, really wanted a girl.

When that was brought to my attention, it made me appreciate him even more. And I know now that Doy Edward Johnson made that secret pledge to himself: that he would always support his children and never tear us down. I know for me personally, it gave me that extra measure of determination I needed to press on.

RJA: *And what about your brother Mike? Did he feel the same way, and was he as good at sports as you?*

Todd: Mike and I were about 18 months apart. So we were extremely close as we were growing up. I was his big-brother/ protector until we got to be about 16 and 14 respectively. After that he shot up like a tree and just dwarfed me.

We have some big men in our family. I'm probably the runt at 6'1". Mike bulked up to about 6'4" and 230 pounds. So when we had our championship football team in our high school, we both played as starters even though Mike was just a sophomore. And yes, he benefitted from my father's discipline and moral support, just as I did. Although it affected each of us differently, I think.

Whatever it was to each individual in our family it worked. In Mike's case, he is the most solid human being I have ever known. He's the one man everyone in his community comes to when they have something that really needs to get done. He is still in Bloomfield and he is one of the pillars of that community.

RJA: *Were you aware of the impact your dad made early on in your life? Or did the realization suddenly kick in later?*

Todd: Originally, when you're a kid, no! At least not consciously! But we always knew he had our back no matter what. If we stepped out of line, there would be hell to pay. But when the chips were down, he was there. And I'm sure it might have made some subliminal impact on my athletic career. Because confidence is a huge factor when you're growing up. And I never felt shortchanged in that department. I've always been fearless, and I definitely have my father to thank for that.

RJA: *I understand you were quite an athlete growing up. Despite what you describe as your "academic indifference" early in life, you were a bit of a small school jock. Baseball, football, golf—quite a resumé!*

Todd: Yes, thank heaven for sports in those days. I guess it made up for some of my other deficiencies at the time. If I couldn't quite figure out what I wanted to do when I grew up, I think I might have wanted to become a professional athlete. I played defensive safety in football on what was a conference championship team in my senior year. And I got some serious scholarship consideration from a few local colleges.

RJA: *Was that your best sport?*

Todd: I was really a good natural golfer and played on the golf team for four years. But my best sport early on was baseball. I played several positions in the field, but what I could really do well was hit. And at an early age I got to be something of a home-run machine—so much so that most of the other Little League and Babe Ruth teams started pitching around me whenever we played them. As I got older my peers caught up to me and surpassed me in every way during high school. All the same I was a starter on our sub-state high school baseball team.

RJA: *That had to be good for your young ego. Did you think you had what it took to go to the big leagues? Or were you that full of yourself?*

Todd: I don't know that I ever thought I would be a big league talent in any sport. (There is such a severe bump up in plateaus of ability even when you jump into college.) But there is no doubt that I was the quintessential arrogant high school jock. So here I was something of a bad boy, an uninspired student at best—but really good at all kinds of athletics—and that made all the difference.

RJA: *But didn't you graduate with honors? I mean you were inducted into the National Honor Society. And that is only for only the best students.*

Todd: Well I did get good grades because Mike and I always got a dollar for every "A" on our report card. So you can call it a cash incentive. It was that important to our parents and (when I think about it) a very smart thing to do. It certainly got the message over to me that *excellence* has its rewards… in a very tangible sense. Besides, it peaked my competitive nature to want to be the best—that meant being the best student—but I was never really driven by a passion for learning, at least not at that point in my life.

RJA: *Then what you're saying is that academics were not your focus; at least not at the time. So I guess you were driven by more basic urges.*

Todd: Sports and girls; hormones and appetites for instant gratification, that pretty well sums it up. I mean, when you grow up in a small Iowa town in the midst of a cluster of other small Iowa towns, sports were almost a religion. So when you're a jock and "a starter" in any number of sports, it becomes the ultimate form of local celebrity, and community activity.

RJA: *You were kind of a campus big shot at that age. And I think that's when you first started dating the lovely Miss Susan Smith— your future bride and mate for life.*

Todd: The first pass anyway. And it didn't last for more than a few dates. She was a couple of grades behind me. So she was really too young, and I was way too wild for her. Her family knew it even if I didn't. I had something of a "bad boy" reputation by that time. Susan's mother certainly didn't approve. And her dad was a 30-year veteran Iowa State Trooper. So here I was, wild as hell, and dating a girl whose father had the legal right to shoot me any time he wanted. When I think about it, that doubtless prompted me to make an early exit from that relationship, and I think Susan's family breathed a genuine sigh of relief to see me go.

RJA: *You're portraying yourself as "wild and crazy guy!" But I've got to ask you really, how wild was that?*

Todd: Well, consider where we grew up. I mean it was Southern Iowa small town wild. And this was the late 1970s and early 1980s. So when kids our age in big cities were smoking grass and dropping acid, our great form of social rebellion was drinking beer underage, drag racing and sneaking out in the middle of the night…just low level mischief and pranks.

I mean by the time I was in high school my dad had gotten a pretty solid job with John Deere, the farm equipment megacorp. So at least we came to be on more solid financial footing.

RJA: *I know your father was a profound influence in your life. Were there others? Coaches? Teachers?*

Todd: My football coach in middle school and high school certainly was. Stan Huggins was what I would call a "player's coach." We could do anything he asked us to do. And he was a tough, no-nonsense guy who was always there when you needed him.

To flavor the sauce of our relationship he had also worked for my father as a younger man, and was a close family friend. So in a way it was like having another uncle around to look after us… and to keep us in line.

RJA: *So was Stan Huggins as much of a disciplinarian as Doy Johnson?*

Todd: Oh very much so. In that regard they were cut from the same cloth. In fact he had this paddle he called "The Charmer." It was all sanded down, smoothed out, and sported air holes and everything. And whatever happened, you did not want to get to know The Charmer.

RJA: *Ah, corporal punishment! Those were the days!*

Todd: I remember one time Coach Huggins overheard me using a couple of four letter swear words in the locker room, and that was something he wouldn't allow. So he brought me in for a session with The Charmer. And I said something like, "OK, I'll let you have 3 licks. But whatever you do, don't tell my dad." As I recall, he gave me 2 and told my dad anyway.

RJA: *Well, it was a very small town. So your father probably would have heard about it eventually. Don't you think?*

Todd: There were very few secrets in Bloomfield. Everybody more or less knew what you had for breakfast, and whenever you had changed the menu. Anyway, Stan was a profound influence in our lives, and is still a great family friend.

Stan Huggins was also one of the best motivators of other people I've ever seen. And yet he did it by keeping things simple. By Stan's measure, the best-conditioned team would always carry the day. So he made sure we were in great shape. He was so inspirational as a coach and so smart as a strategist that our defense on the high school football team would run through walls for him. I think we only had 20 points scored on us my entire senior year. In fact, I'm sure we would have won the state championship if our star quarterback Mike Rupe hadn't gotten injured the week before the last game of the season.

RJA: *Mike Rupe was one of your best friends growing up, as I recall.*

Todd: Yes he was. Mike was a terrific guy. He was very much a part of what we did at that age. He was a great natural athlete. And I think if he hadn't had that injury in the last game of the regular season, he probably would have gotten some scholarship offers to major schools, and some kind of extended career—at least through college.

RJA: *Life has this way of twisting fate whether we like it or not. I think there is a Yiddish Proverb that Woody Allen more or less took credit for: "If you want to make God laugh tell him your plans."*

Todd: Funny, but I'm not sure I agree. I also believe that God rewards intention. If you have a purpose and a passion, the universe knows and rewards you for it.

RJA: *And that goes back to Emerson as we discussed. So who helped instill that passion to begin with? You've mentioned that you didn't really catch on about that until you were in college.*

Todd: My first glimpse of that probably came with another major male influence in my life up to that point, my great uncle Don Prevo. I know I had mentioned Uncle Don earlier. He was my father's mother's brother (my paternal grandmother). And he was this almost legendary figure from the very rich Chicago suburb of Winnetka, Illinois. To the rest of the family, he was like the Wizard of Oz or something.

He was very tall and a physically imposing man but always gifted with a vibrancy that made you feel more alive just being around him. He was always there for everybody. And even though I didn't know him well in the beginning, he always made me feel as if he took a special personal interest in me.

He probably made other people feel that way as well, because that was just his nature—expansive, generous, outgoing, there to leave an impact that always made you sense life at a deeper level.

One thing he inspired me to do from the very moment I met him was to always think big, always to go that extra mile. He was a risk-taker and he motivated me to be the same way. It was a matter of legend that he was a self-made millionaire. I'll go into the fascinating account of how he did that later, because we spent a great deal of time together when I went to work for him during the summer of my last year of college. But what he did for me very early, even when I was a young boy, was to repeatedly stress the fact that it was essential to set goals and to pursue those goals with everything you have.

In a way, it was as if Uncle Don wanted to see whether or not you would take a step or two toward taking charge of your own life before he would come to your side with a bunch of aid and good advice. In my case that relationship jumped to an even higher level once I got into college, and he saw that I was on a solid life's path of my own choosing.

RJA: *And wasn't he the one who first peaked your interest in Hedge apples?*

Todd: For the most part, that came later, when he knew that I was about to embrace a course of study in science and specifically in chemistry. Then he really made an emphasis of that. But yes! Even in the early days when I was around fifteen, we would pass a grove of hedge apple trees and he would take note of them and say, "There is some magic in those little green balls."

Of course, everyone probably thought he was being a bit eccentric. But I could also tell that at a very deep level he was serious. And if I had ever learned two things about my great uncle Don over the years it was the he had remarkable instincts. And he never brought up anything unless he had given it a great deal of thought.

It also struck me as curious at the time that the squirrels and deer, using Nature's sonar, somehow managed to smash into these big green balls and eat the seeds. So that curious kind of foraging was something that stuck with me over the years. And it would reintroduce itself in a very big way about twenty years later.

RJA: *So the hedge ball thing stuck with you, in the corners of your consciousness.*

Todd: They were always there, a part of the landscape and always this kind of castoff of nature. Farmers didn't want them. You saw them in the hedgerows and gullies of small farms, just lying there decomposing. Still, there they were always around, a part of our Midwestern landscape. And at some level, Uncle Don's autosuggestion implants always managed to claw away in the corners of my consciousness.

RJA: *Probably not a great concern to you by the time you got through high school. And I note that, as a young high school senior you seemed to have everything going your way. A three-sport letterman—foot-*

ball, baseball and golf—a super popular jock, and you had decided to go to college at that point...on a scholarship of sorts.

Todd: Yes, that was a bit unusual. First I had decided to go to college probably just because it was the thing to do at the time. I also remembered my dad, who never had the best education, stressing to me the importance of it. And I had this rather unusual scholarship offer from a small Division III liberal arts university called Coe College.

Coe was located in Cedar Rapids, Iowa. Cedar Rapids was the second largest township in the state of Iowa and had a population of about 130,000 people. So that made it the biggest city I had ever seen at the time. I got thousands of dollars in tuition money and free dorm space on what amounted to a quasi-academic scholarship, with the understanding that I would play on their football team.

RJA: *Actually Coe has garnered a pretty good academic reputation in the last 30 years or so.*

Todd: Nice to know, but it was totally lost on me at the time. My freshman year at Coe was what I have to call "The Lost Year." Because this was a time when I did nothing but drink, party and chase girls and basically do the classic college playboy thing. (Although I certainly didn't have the money to be a proper playboy.)

Due to an injury and a pretty strange string of events, I ended up never playing a down of football at Coe, and I don't think I ever even attended a workout. So in a way I was more or less in violation of my scholarship agreement. And that started to gnaw at me. My grades suffered. I think I made a 2.5 grade point average out of a possible 4.0. So, academically, I was a living testament to mediocrity, and basically in every sense of the phrase I could think of I was just a mess.

RJA: *Surely you had to take away something of value from that year, other than learning what not to do and what didn't work. Was there any one thing you remember that made a difference?*

Todd: Yes there was one specific occasion that I remember. And that was an elective science course I took—The History of Science—that I was more or less drawn to. And toward the end of the semester I wrote a paper on the course that netted me a B-minus or something; but that wasn't what did it for me. It was the comment on the cover sheet by my Professor Sandford, and it went something like this: "You have a brilliant mind. You have a real gift for this. Too bad you don't have the discipline to take it to its fullest potential." Frankly, I have to admit, it stung a little. Because I instinctively knew that he was right.

RJA: *Something did, because by the next year you had managed to get into the University of Iowa, paid your tuition and started working two jobs to put yourself through school. Not an easy undertaking by any measure. So…what turned the corner for you? Was there a tipping point?*

Todd: Well, I guess there were several. And they all seemed to click into place right around the same time. First, I came back for summer break after the end of my first year at Coe, having accomplished virtually nothing. My scholarship money (justifiably) evaporated. So I was starting all over again with nothing.

Fortunately, I successfully applied to the University of Iowa and was accepted (essentially on the basis of my decent transcripts from high school). But I had no money. So I was confronted with the prospect of having to work my way through school.

My dad had always instilled in me this Code of Conduct: ("Excellence is when you do your best when no one is looking.") And I realized that my social peccadilloes and carousing were just a flat waste of time, finally remembering somewhere along the way what Coach (Stan) Huggins used to tell us all: "Don't become a jackass once the sun goes down."

Now I was in Iowa City at the University of Iowa and working at least 30 hours a week to pay for books and tuition. So I decided there and then that as long as I was pounding away this hard to get a quality education, I should really apply myself and make some very good grades.

I still hadn't picked out a career path for myself. So I was staying on a Liberal Arts curriculum, but I decided to be that guy.

RJA: *That guy?*

Todd: Sure, *that guy:* the one with all the mojo, the one who became an academic role model for others. So I decided to become a scholar with all means at my disposal. I've always been compulsive about accomplishing anything. So I became OCD about being smart and kicking butt in college.

I was working about 30 hours a week and 60 hours a week during the summer. Every other spare moment I had I devoted to studying and devouring all the information I could get on any given subject. And to no one's surprise, the minute I committed to that, everything started to change. I came into that positive feedback loop where you draw into you all the things you truly want in life.

RJA: *The Law of Attraction invariably comes into play. And it seems at that point as if you more or less set a template for the rest of your life. Was there an event or a series of events that might have triggered things as well?*

Todd: I truly believe things tend to tumble into place once you reset the direction of your life. So Several connections, I think came into play for me once I decided to embrace my academic career with a new kind of resolution. And for the most part they turned out to be lifetime connections on the highest possible plane.

The first had to be my connection with my chemistry professor at the University of Iowa, Dr. Lou Messerle. I was already gravitating toward a complete immersion in science by my second year at the U of I when I came upon this up and coming superstar in the fields of both organic and inorganic chemistry.

Lou Messerle was an Associate Professor of Chemistry at the time. He was a graduate of Brown University, got his PhD in Chemistry at MIT and did his post doctorate in the Society of Fellows at the University of Michigan. In the process of doing all that he had become something of a forerunner in the field of organometallic chemistry.

RJA: *That's quite a laundry list of credentials. Did he live up to them?*

Todd: Every bit of that and more so. He instilled such a passion in you to do your best, to dig deeper and to go for solutions—no matter what the challenge. More important, he saw that raw talent in me that I probably didn't even see in myself...and not only encouraged me to develop it, he showed me how "the sausage was made."

RJA: *So how was "the sausage" made? I know that's code for how things work. But what was it about Lou Messerle that made his work with you so special?*

Todd: I think the thing about Lou Messerle that made him so special (and still does) was the fact that he has always been able to weave a credible universe beyond the mere math and formulation that comprises your early experiences in chemistry and science. He had a way of revealing the end result in ways that made it all seem worthwhile.

Rather than just get lost in theory and formulation, you engaged in the sheer joy of discovery. That went a long way into getting me impassioned over a career in applied chemistry. From there, Lou certainly encouraged me to dive all the way down into the deep end of the pool and get my graduate degree.

RJA: *He was the prime mover in your career decisions to that point. So how else did he influence you?*

Todd: Lou sent me away from Iowa after earning my BS in Chemistry with honors and stressed that I should attend either Indiana or Purdue University as a Ph.D. research candidate. And no question, Lou Messerle was also instrumental in encouraging me toward getting my PhD in Chemistry at Indiana University, and did whatever he could to help see me accepted into that program.

RJA: *So, backing up a bit, here you were, still an undergrad. And everything seemed to be shifting in the direction of your "destiny." You made a close lifelong friend there as well. Isn't that where you first met Erik Tjaden? And wasn't he in the same chemistry program with you at Iowa?*

Todd: I met Erik as an undergrad at the University of Iowa. We were both chemistry majors and shared many of the same interests. In other ways we could not have been more different. Here I was a jock and an extrovert, a natural networker—always out front with my questions and fearless in my dealings with others. And Erik was much more reserved, something of an introvert and a bit shy. I was all bravado and oozing confidence (and occasionally over the top about it) while Erik was almost pointedly low profile. All the while, he was quite brilliant and broadly accomplished. In fact, he played the cello with a virtuoso skill.

It also seemed that we connected in areas that really mattered—our sense of focus on what was important and, I like to think, a shared sense of values where our work and our word were concerned.

I think he tended to enjoy the fact that I was able to get him out of his conservative cocoon at times, and so we both learned how to work hard when it mattered, and play just as hard when it didn't.

The other way in which we were complete opposites lay in the fact that I was a poor boy working his way up from the trailer courts of Southeastern Iowa, while Erik came from a world of privilege. Not that he ever flaunted it to anyone, but I remember that he had a cello bow (probably a Stradivarius) that cost about the same as a Rolls Royce Silver Cloud. His father was a urologist of some local renown. And yet I was very touched by the way the Tjadens instantly accepted me, opening their home to me and embracing me as one of the family.

RJA: *So this was a lifetime relationship from that point on. You went on to room together in graduate school at Indiana. You became business partners and working associates on several occasions. And he is your partner now in all things Pomifera.*

Todd: Yes, he's the principal funding source and silent partner in the company. I think he is the very definition of a loyal friend, and a great business partner. Thus far we have gone all the way together. He even stood up as a groomsman when I married Susan.

RJA: *Which leads me to the third part of this rather significant triumvirate in your life: Your very accomplished wife: Susan Smith Johnson.*

Todd: Right. I married the woman of my dreams, and she still can't get a check cashed without showing some ID. (And that's probably the only drawback to what has otherwise turned out to be the best decision of my life—to convince this very special soul to spend the rest of her life with me.)

RJA: *So you reconnected with Susan when you were at the University of Iowa, and this time it was quite an improvement over your* *first experience. So I guess you had both grown up a little by then. And what: the chemistry was better?*

Todd: I think the chemistry was probably always good. It's just that she was not yet fully grown the first time, and I was sort of flying out of control and enjoying every minute of it. When we connected later on during my junior year at Iowa, what I saw before me was a woman fully in command of herself—gentle but strong, quiet but utterly in control of her purpose in life. And seeing that kind of quiet confidence, that serene sense of self in a woman of any age, is a genuine turn-on.

By the time I started dating Susan a second time, she had become a woman in full. She was shapely. She was beautiful. To me she was hot. She was mature, especially for someone 19 years of age. And she had some very clear goals. (She was going to be an RN/BSN and also get her MS as a Nurse Practitioner in the process. That was a lot on the plate for a woman of that age. And yet she never wavered in her determination to do it.)

By that time I had gone through a run of proverbial toxic relationships, each one crazier than the one before, and was truly delighted to reconnect with this woman who was something of a straight arrow. By the same token she was enough aware of herself to let a sense of adventure slip into her life.

More important, at this point, we clicked in all the right places. What struck me somewhere along the way in our next year of being together was the fact that she brought me back to center every time. We connected with that kind of mental and emotional shorthand that two people make when they have complete rapport.

I loved her and I trusted her, and knew I could do so with my life. So, in the course of the next five years, I came to the decision that this was the woman I wanted to spend the rest of my life with.

RJA: *But you only dated at first. And you moved in together when you were in grad school at Indiana. So it didn't all happen over night, did it?*

Todd: No it didn't. It was a journey – with this wonderful cast of characters – that took place over the course of several years. Susan and I would eventually move in together. Erik would actually room with us for a short time. We all became a kind of family. Even after he moved on to his own curriculum, which differed somewhat from my own, we always kept the connection, socialized on weekends, had a couple of double-dates and spent a great deal of time sharing time and space and dreams.

RJA: *So I suppose this sort of sets the table for the rest of your coursings through the halls of academia in the University of Iowa, Indiana University and your post doctoral work at the University of Utah in Salt Lake City. I mean you had six to eight more years of hard study, trial and error and challenges to rededicate yourself and eventually achieve your PhD. Did you ever doubt yourself?*

Todd: I suppose every man doubts his course of action from time to time. If so, it was only momentary. And for the most part, my determination and optimism always took over. Besides, by this time I had that woman in my life—that significant other self, that soul mate—that gave me both the anchor and the backbone to see it through.

RJA: *So I have to surmise by now that your father, your mother and your great Uncle Don were quite proud to see the direction your life was taking.*

Todd: Yes they were. And I'm glad you brought up Uncle Don again. Because I get to close the loop on this part of the story with a very special summer I spent working in Chicago prior to my senior year at Iowa. I was still working 30 and 35 hours a week putting myself through school and studying another 50 hours a week when he invited me in June of 1986 to come and work for him.

Uncle Don had always kept his eye on me over the years while I was growing up. We had talked on the phone from time to time, and I always sensed that he was more or less charting my progress. He was wonderfully outgoing and always gently nudged me to up the level of my game at whatever I was doing.

Even so, he was still this legend of sorts—that very rich Great Uncle Don, far away in the fancy Beverly Hills of Chicago (Winnetka, Illinois). Rumor was, he had a mansion with an elevator in it. And everyone thought of him as something like a combination of Andrew Carnegie and the Wizard of OZ, whose wife was (appropriately) named Dorothy.

Finally, when I went out to work for uncle Don during that summer of '86, and stayed in the house with him and aunt Dorothy I discovered something even more endearing: a flesh and blood man who was very accessible, very human and with a terrific backstory all his own.

I knew Uncle Don had been a World War II veteran who came back from that terrible global conflict expecting to reboot his life by tapping into the small savings he'd amassed before he left…only to find out to his horror that his own father had kited the funds, leaving him virtually penniless.

Such a discovery and betrayal might have left a lesser man devastated, but Don Prevo looked upon it as a challenge to his ingenuity. And over the years he built up a blood-laboratory business that was unique and very much in demand. He was very much the entrepreneur and made sure that I too understood how important it was to innovate and be entrepreneurial in everything I did. And I was delighted when he invited me to come and work for him during the summer before my senior year at the University of Iowa.

Uncle Don made sure I earned every cent during that summer, but he also paid me so well ($15 an hour at that time) that I managed to garner enough cash to pay for my entire senior year at Iowa. That freed me up to do so many extraordinary things in that final pivotal two semesters in school.

It was also during that summer that Uncle Don spent a lot of time acting as my mentor. I mean, he never did it by cramming his wisdom and knowledge down your throat. But he was a great guide, and he led by example.

He was a master of networking. He had a gift for building long-lasting relationships, and taught me the real value of "paying it forward." And I mean that in the classic sense: doing good things for others will always come back to you a thousand fold.

RJA: *The Laws of Karma…and building your network by surrounding yourself with good people. Makes all the sense in the world when you think about it.*

Todd: To be sure. Don Prevo was also very much a risk taker. He always dealt with life in the most expansive terms. He dreamt big dreams. He saw those qualities in me and convinced me that I could make that translation in anything I did. And he gave me some pointers on how to do it effectively that were priceless by any measure.

RJA: *And I suppose he also kept setting in those Pomifera implants, didn't he? That seemed to be something of a cause celébre for him.*

Todd: Yes, he was very consistent and unequivocal about that. Especially knowing that my field of study was going to be a graduate degree in Chemistry, he saw the fit. "There's something magical about those hedge balls," he kept up the mantra. He said it often, and as it turned out I'm awfully glad he did.

RJA: *And didn't he encourage you to experiment with them in the labs?*

Todd: Yes he did. But that little chain of events didn't take place until I was getting my PhD at Indiana University. And that's another story that we'll cut into later on…literally ☺

> *My brother is the smartest guy I know.*
> *He also has this wonderful quality of*
> *never taking himself too seriously.*
>
> **~ Mike Johnson**

CHAPTER 3

AN EDUCATED MAN

"A lot of people do a lot of talking without a single brain in their head. What they do have that you haven't got is a diploma. Therefore by virtue of the power invested in me… I hereby grant you the honorary degree of ThD… Doctor of Thinkology!"

— The Wizard of Oz (to the Scarecrow)

Todd Johnson learned a long time ago the value of credentials. They are leverage to the greater good and what he jokingly refers to as "the keys to the executive washroom."
Todd is a fan of the *Wizard of Oz,* and I note the appropriateness of our reference to both the book and the man for any number of reasons: First, it was the nickname his family gave their legendary Great Uncle Don Prevo. Second, I personally cannot help but note some stream of connection between "Uncle Don," Todd Johnson himself and the author and creator of the Oz series of books, Frank L. Baum, because all three men "boot-strapped" their way into becoming remarkably successful.

"We've already told the better part of my great uncle's success story," Todd notes, over a quick energy snack. "And I'm still a work in progress. But what I didn't know until you told me just what a long climb to success Frank L. Baum had to take to get the *Wizard of Oz* series to become the success it was."

Todd got the reference, because what very few people realize is that 21 publishers turned down Frank L. Baum's original manuscript of *[The Wonderful World of]* the *Wizard of Oz.* It was such a resounding consensus of rejection that Baum decided to publish the first book himself. He believed in the purpose and mission of his series. For the first year the book was printed (in 1900) Baum actually sold it out of the back of his wagon, travelling to bookstores to build demand. The rest is legend, because *The Wizard of Oz,* and the entire Oz book/film series went on to sell over 20 million copies (and 14 Oz books) before it went into public domain in 1956, on the way to becoming a literary legend.

I make the comparison to Todd and Pomifera®. And in a way that makes him laugh, I note that no one believed in Pomifera® and what it could do until Todd Johnson came along. And he is the first to acknowledge that had he not brought a PhD in Chemistry and a portfolio of patents into the mix, the miracle of the One Drop Wonder™ might never have seen the light of day.

So, that's the first question I hit Todd with during this set of interviews. And, as usual, he gets it right away.

RJA: *By now, I'm sure you realize that your credentials and your degrees as a scientist of some renown have enabled you to create this company.*

Todd: And that's an inconvenient truth. People, companies, networks and governments all respect that PhD after your name, if for no other reason than the fact that it tells them, you've paid your dues to get here. So you're not just some hack fooling around in his garage.

RJA: *Is that what prompted you do go for the degree? Certainly it had to be at least part of the payoff at the other end of your goals and objectives.*

Todd: Chock at least part of it up to my competitive nature. I was out to be among the best academically. But the other facet of it made sense as well, because a PhD in my course of study is something like winning an Olympic Gold Medal—in this case, the Science Olympics.

RJA: *In a way you did, which is a topic we can cover in a minute. But I wanted to get to that prime motivation that caused you to turn the corner. From what we've discussed, it seems to point to the period when you were at the University of Iowa studying under your professor Dr. Lou Messerle.*

Todd: Right. The real arrival at "crossover dreams" came to me in my junior year at Iowa. And it came at two levels: At one level, I had gone from being pretty good at chemistry and my other science courses to becoming what Lou acknowledged as "something very special." (His words.) That meant a lot to me. But more than that it prompted me to make a series of decisions that would set the course for the rest of my life.

RJA: *Ah, the defining moment!*

Todd: …Or "moments" in this case. In the case of Dr. Lou Messerle, the impact was stellar in so many ways. He was an associate professor when I was at Iowa. And yet he had his own team of handpicked superstar students (of which I was honored to be one) in what they referred to as the Messerle Research Group. They have groups like this inside the Science Departments at Iowa, but his was one of the most prestigious.

So what I guess Lou saw in me was what he fondly referred to as "a diamond in the rough." He liked my penchant for higher-end concepts and risk-taking and the fact that I was a quick study when it came to problem solving. What I mean by that was an ability I had to see something and figure it out. Whether it was a problem or an experiment, I could arrive at the correct answer without necessarily hacking my way through the thicket to get there.

RJA: *That's kind of qualitative analysis, isn't it? I mean you can arrive at the right conclusion even though you've skipped some of the steps on the Ladder of Inference.*

Todd: As opposed to quantitative analysis and lumbering through every single step…yes!

RJA: *That's quite a quantum leap in problem solving.*

Todd: Not all academics see it that way. But Lou Messerle did. He saw that ability in me as a gift, and he was the first to reinforce my self worth and say to me: "You know Todd, you should really get a PhD in Chemistry." It took a while for it to sink in. But given my almost congenital drive to be the best at anything, his words of encouragement inspired me just to go for it.

RJA: *You said it came at two levels. What was the second level?*

Todd: Well, the other inspiration was my own wife, Susan. By my junior year, we were very involved and becoming committed to one another. And here is this woman two years my junior who was focused and mature…and determined to get her degree not only as an RN/BSN (Registered Nurse/Bachelors of Science in Nursing) but also go after her MS in nursing. Seeing Susan that dedicated and determined even that early in her career clearly inspired me.

Susan has always had that effect on me, and when I confided to her that I thought I was going to try for my PhD in Chemistry, she was 1000% behind me on it, and in fact encouraged me to do so. She has always been that person—that other piece in the puzzle of me. In every imaginable sense of the word (and thank you *Jerry Maguire*), "she completes me."

I also have to add to that a footnote that it was also around that time that my best friend in college Erik Tjaden had also decided to go for his doctorate in chemistry. Because Erik was also part of the Messerle Research Group, I knew he had made his commitment early on to go for a PhD. So that also had a triggering effect on my desire to do so.

RJA: *It seems to me you probably would have anyway.*

Todd: I'm sure I would have as well. But that more or less put the icing on the cake. And it reinforced my conviction that I was on the right path at the time. What was overwhelming to me was how excited Erik's parents were when we announced we were going to attend Indiana University. That kind of validation from the Tjadens cemented the fact I could achieve incredible things in academia.

RJA: *So you were accepted into Indiana University's Chemistry PhD program in January of 1988. And by all evidence, that wasn't an easy thing to do.*

Todd: No, in fact I was one of a handful selected out of hundreds of applicants for an off semester admittance, and I'm sure it was because I had a few things working in my favor. One was a run of recommendations from the right people, including Lou Messerle (who constantly encouraged me to do this). Another was the fact that I had a rather shiny grade average by that time. I had also written a pretty decent set of academic papers to get me in front of the decision makers. And one's ability to communicate—especially at the graduate level—always works in your favor.

RJA: *And was Erik Tjaden another one accepted? I notice that he ended up going to Indiana University for his PhD as well. Were you in fact classmates?*

Todd: Yes we were classmates at Iowa and now going to be roommates at Indiana. So there I was in a whole new university atmosphere in Bloomington, Indiana and with a pretty prestigious set of professors, the most significant of whom was Dr. Ken Caulton, who was another pivotal influence in my academic career.

People don't realize it, but it's true. It's a tradition started at Oxford, I believe, where aspiring graduates were placed according to merit with certain tutors, mentors and fellows and allowed to grow from there. Here we call them thesis advisors. And Dr. Caulton was my thesis advisor when I was at Indiana. As you can imagine, these people exert a powerful influence in your life. You're inside their tent for several years. And if you're lucky, as I was, it was the perfect place to be.

RJA: *What was it about Dr. Caulton that made him so exceptional?*

Todd: If I had to put it in a word it might be *refinement*. Where Lou Messerle saw the form I came to him as a diamond in the rough—determined, inspired and directed but still a bit rough around the edges. I think he made me a better tougher diamond, but one with a bit more polish.

Ken Caulton took me to that next level. I was something of a bulldozer when I got into Indiana's PhD program. I had worked so hard to get to the highest levels in my chemistry studies at Iowa that I may have showed up at Indiana with something of a chip on my shoulder. I was so fired up when I hit the door there, I was ready to ram through a brick wall to get things done if I had to. Ken Caulton showed me how to build a ladder to climb over the top of that wall—the course of action that causes less breakage and achieves a longer lasting result. So Ken was the one who introduced me to a paradigm shift in problem solving.

RJA: *An art form if there ever was one. So...did he count you as an elite member of his core group? Or did you earn his respect the old fashioned way—by working for it?*

Todd: Well, it had to be a bit of both. In the first place you were in the 1% category even to get inside the building. So I was already in the AA+ bracket when I showed up. What these phenomenal people do is get you to a level you didn't even know was there. And in Ken Caulton's case, he led by example. He was a true role model and a genuine Renaissance man. He was multilingual, fluent in about 4 languages and conversant in a couple more. He was a published poet and something of a master of classical music.

When I was exposed to all the things he had done with his life, it just made me want to be a better, more refined, human being. And at this level you had to dig deeper and work harder just to keep up. You can't put a dollar value on that kind of exposure...and the experiences that come out of it.

RJA: *And Erik Tjaden reached that level as well.*

Todd: Yes, because of Erik's professional upbringing, from my point of view, he transitioned so easily into the rigors of advanced scientific study. As Erik was excellent at all things, he was also a superb student. And yes he was there inside the same laboratory environment with me but in a different research group and thesis advisor. Nevertheless, we shared a lot of lab projects, a good many study slots and a small cluster social weekends together at the infamous "Quarry" just outside Bloomington.* It was a very special period in my life.

RJA: *I noticed when I researched Dr. Caulton that he has his own lab group with its own website inside the IU umbrella. That seems very much like a fiefdom of sorts inside the Kingdom of Academia. Something of a medieval metaphor, I admit...*

---

* The Quarry, is a popular Indiana swimming hole made famous in the 1987 cycling film *Breaking Away*.

Todd: But accurate, I think. Ken Caulton was very much a superstar at IU, and yes! That's the way these people are allowed to operate inside the doctoral curriculum. For me, it was also personal. He truly became another father figure for me.

One indelible imprint he made in my life was encouraging me to refine the discipline of the Proper Scientific Method.

RJA: *So there is actually a step-by-step aspect to this? I suppose I shouldn't be surprised about that. It's only logical.*

Todd: It's also surprising when you find out that it doesn't always happen inside other groups, or other programs. And yet under Ken Caulton's science umbrella, it was absolutely essential. It's a practical procedure when you think about it. But parts of it were unique to this man's approach to chemistry, and the steps go something like this:

First you work on critical thinking. That begins with an open mind. See all possibilities and set them up in front of you.

Second you use scientific methods to set up your test model.

That requires the *third step—eliminating bias.* That's a tough one, because everybody tends to bring the prejudice of previous experience into the test.

But once you follow *step four, setting up your controls, you get to see how it all pays off.* You *double-check your data* and then *triple check your interpretation.* Those are *steps five and six,* which leads to the *final step* where you come to *present your results.*

So much traditional lab work is induction, where a theory is set in place and researchers try to form a result around it. Dr. Caulton's critical method required an extensive application of deduction, and that made all the difference. In terms of methodology it was the scientific equivalent of Sherlock Holmes vs. Inspector Clouseau.

RJA: *Was it hard to adjust to? It seems to go so much against the grain of so many disciplines.*

Todd: What was difficult for me was to open my mind and think about how to test certain hypotheses that Ken had.

RJA: *Was it a grind? I mean there had to be some days when repetition of steps and going through certain disciplines had to seem like an endless loop. Did it ever drive you crazy?*

Todd: I don't think you really have time to think about that. You get so absorbed into the process that you just get into *that zone.* What I did get to realize later if not immediately was this: what you sew in the labs during one season, you reap the harvest for in another. It all pays off in the end, and it especially paid off when I was experimenting with Pomifera®...and in ways that I might have never believed possible. But hey! That's chemistry!

RJA: *Speaking of Chemistry! All this time you were successfully merging your life with the lovely Miss Susan Smith—and doing so in a way that eventually led to marriage.*

Todd: Nice segue...

RJA: *Had to be tough, at least logistically, wasn't it? Not only were you working your way through graduate school, and working in the Caulton Lab Group, you and Susan also managed to deepen your* *relationship. Working and studying about 100 hours a week, where did you find the time?*

Todd: It wasn't easy. But I have to tell you something I've discovered about myself over the years: The more you give me to do, the more it inspires me to get it done. It's as if all that time-demand super-generates a new kind of momentum for me that just synergizes into something even more productive. For some reason I feed on it, and it challenges me to find even more creative ways to do it. Where Susan was concerned I had reached that rare point in that special relationship when you just know this is the person that you have to be with for the rest of your life. So nothing was going to keep me from that. Fortunately, she felt the same way I did. So we made it work.

RJA: *Walk me through that if you don't mind. Because for a while you are at different universities...and than you weren't. She was working and you had decided to move in together. So what was it about Susan that just made you realize that she was the one?*

Todd: Well, beyond the obvious fact that she was very attractive, very bright and very kind—the irresistible trifecta—she was also in terms of pure psychodynamics one of the strongest women I had ever met.

I'm very much an extrovert, as you have no doubt determined by now. I'm also enthusiastic and aggressive in my passion, sometimes to a fault. So, often without meaning to, I just steamroll over a good many people. With Susan, I realized that was never going to happen. Very kind but also very firm in her personal values, she never backs down when she knows she's right. So on a very personal level Susan can hold her own with anybody.

After a while in our relationship, she had a beautiful way of putting me in my place. She would just back off, look me in the eye and say: "You know, you're really not as awesome as you think you are."

RJA: *That's a pretty strong pair of personalities. Was there ever a power struggle?*

Todd: Not really. First of all there was a great deal of mutual respect almost from the beginning. So anytime we've had differences we have always been able to work them out. I know she believes in me, and she is my anchor. So there is a bond of trust that is unbreakable. Second, living with three very smart, accomplished women as I have over the years (my wife and two daughters Emily and Leah) you have to realize there are a lot of times when they're going to outsmart you.

RJA: *So, are you saying that you believe in the Natural Superiority of Women?*

Todd: Ha ha! (Is that a trick question?) That's another conversation for another time. But what you do get with the kind of relationship I have with Susan is what psychologist Nathaniel Branden once described in *The Psychology of Self Esteem* as the Mathematics of Synergy—that in a love relationship 1 + 1 almost never equals 2. It is either more than 2 in a great relationship; or, if the relationship is toxic, it is less than 2. Susan and I together are definitely more than 2. And that makes all the difference.

RJA: *So would you say you are a lot alike? I mean, from what I've seen of you two, I don't think so. But appearances can be deceiving.*

Todd: We're alike to the degree that we very much share the same values. And we reach for the same levels of integrity. So, in all the ways that matter yes! Otherwise, we couldn't be more different. I'm more or less the ultimate Alpha male—outgoing, adventuresome, willing to go where angels fear to tread.

Although Susan is probably what you would call an ambivert (because she can get along with people wonderfully well when she needs to), she is a great deal quieter and more soft-spoken in the way she moves about her day. Still she is equally comfortable on her own and generally leaves the limelight to me (every pun intended). At the same time, she always pulls me back to center when I get a little too far "out there." She is my consummate reality check about life. She's always around to remind me to "get real."

RJA: *Rare indeed is that kind of relationship. So I can see why you'd want to hold fast to that. So… how did you manage?*

Todd: Well by my second year in graduate school at IU, Susan had gotten her BSN (from Iowa) and had taken a job as an RN in Bloomington, Indiana. So it was close enough for us to move in together in an apartment near the university.

At that point, Susan worked night shifts at (the hospital) that ran from 11 p.m. to 7 a.m. And when she did, I would go into the lab during night hours and run lab tests and testing protocols until the wee hours of the morning. That way we were more or less on the same schedule. So we were creatively disruptive in the way that we managed to arrange our lives…and we just found a way to make it work.

RJA: *Were there ever problems…or challenges?*

Todd: Part of living, I suppose. But there was never a challenge Susan and I couldn't work through. Our love was strong, despite the busy schedules. And it's always tough when one partner in a marriage is working and the other is working *and* pounding his way through a PhD program…in Chemistry of all things. That's all an energy drain. But we were young. And as I said earlier, for some perverse reason, the more action there is for me, the better I like it. I do remember, getting in trouble one time, however, and wouldn't you know, it all had something to do with Pomifera®.

RJA: *Ah, a foreshadowing of things to come. Can you relate?*

Todd: Well, it's here where I once again bring in my legendary "Wizard of Oz" Great Uncle Don, who had become more involved with my life the older and more focused I came to be. I knew how proud he was of me, especially in my pursuit of the higher levels of academia. He had told me so on several occasions, and had always encouraged me with offers of financial help and moral support whenever I needed it.

Then in the autumn of 1990, which was my third year in the Indiana University doctorate program, Uncle Don once again planted the seed for me to look for that special something inside those "little green balls," as he liked to call them.

I had to give the old boy credit. Once he believed he was right about something, he held onto it with both hands and a sharp set of teeth. And Pomifera® was definitely a cause celébre for him.

So here we were near the end of the autumn of 1990 when Uncle Don actually drove over from Chicago with a jumbo sack filled with hedge-apples and subsequently smooth-talked me into having a go at chemically breaking down a batch of them.

I think Susan was on shift that night, but Uncle Don takes us out to a nice dinner and very politely implants the long held conviction that he thinks I am the one who can get on top of this whole concept.

I think he said, "If anyone can do this, you can," or something else sufficiently flattering to coax me into it. And so I took the bait.

RJA: *Was it bait? I mean he didn't really trap you, did he? You were what I would have to describe as a "warm market." So I assume you were ready to take it on.*

Todd: Well… originally I just did it to be polite. He was such a sweet old guy, and he was so invested in his belief in this whole concept that I couldn't let him down. At that point at Indiana I was on a roll with some big wins in the lab. So I thought I might actually be able to extract some findings from a few simple tests. But looking back on it now, I really didn't have enough tools in my bag to pull it off. So the following comedy of errors probably saved me from what would have, at that point, amounted to a huge waste of time.

RJA: *Comedy of errors? In what way?*

Todd: A genuine "mad scientist" *Back to the Future* moment. So to tell the story, you have to remember that hedge apples are impossibly tough little pieces of Mother Nature's seasonal cast-offs; they're such a clutter they're virtually looked upon as a glorified weed. And before we came along, they actually had arboreal programs on how to dispose of them. (Even Martha Stewart had some recommendations for this!)

They can range in size from tennis balls to slow pitch softballs and are extremely hard. I've seen kids use them for batting practice and never even crack one. They're pretty good to play catch with, but they have this sticky resin that gets all over everything. So in a way they have always been just a kind of gummy balled-up nuisance.

Trust me there were plenty of them. Uncle Don had seen to that. So here I was with a bunch of hedge apples that I had to slice up. That was tough enough. But the problem with them has always been that they were so durable and so hard, you had to soften them up by exposing them to a bit of heat before you would really make any qualitative extractions—so I thought anyway.

Then, armed to the teeth with cocksure ignorance, and a boatload of second hand knowledge I stuck them in the oven and set it on *Warm* to tenderize them a bit.

RJA: *OMG, I see it coming…*

Todd: Well, I wish I had. Because I set the oven at 275° or something and turned off the oven because I needed to work up a reaction at the lab. And while I was gone, Susan comes home and wants to start cooking a roast. So she preheats the oven to 425°

and then she leaves the room for a while. Well, the next thing you know the kitchen is reeking and when Susan goes in to see what happened...oh wow!

First the stench was terrible. (You *do not* want to roast hedge apples!) But worse than that was what we discovered once we opened the oven door.

RJA: *I can only imagine.*

Todd: You know the scene in *Ghostbusters* when Bill Murray's character gets "slimed" by the electro-charged ectoplasmic spook—the bilious green ooze and muck that resembles a pile of mucous. Triple that! That took some explaining, I can tell you. And Susan still gives me a hard time about it once in a while.

RJA: *I bet you wish you'd put up a Post-it™ note on the oven door.*

Todd: To say the least. But, needless to say, that tabled any Pomifera® experiments for a decade or two.

RJA: *And your domestic tranquility? How did that fare after that?*

Todd: Like all truly good relationships, it gave us a lot to laugh about once we managed to clean up the mess, which took a day or two and a lot of elbow grease.

RJA: *So, were you married at that time?*

Todd: Oh yes! Susan and I had been married about a year and a half by then. The year before, she had graduated from the University of Iowa with her RN/BSN. And I was rooming with Erik

Tjaden at Indiana for a while. So when I asked her to come out and live with me, she proved once again to be that straight-arrow traditionalist and said, "Not going to happen unless you promise to marry me first."

And so I did. I already wanted very much to do so. So, it was a done deal. And to cap this life altering decision, I actually did it the old-fashioned way. I paid Susan's father a visit and asked for her hand in marriage.

RJA: *And how did he take it? Or did he still see you as the wild card oddball boyfriend in his daughter's life?*

Todd: No, but by then I think I'd earned his grudging respect. Because when I went to him and asked his permission for Susan's hand in marriage, he responded in a rather classic fashion... something like, "Well, it's about G**D*** time..." or words to that effect. That was "Smitty" (Susan's dad) and a classic response coming from him.

So I guess you'd have to say, he finally accepted me.

RJA: *So you got married on May 27, 1989, which I understand was the same as Susan's parent's anniversary. How did that happen?*

Todd: Just happened to fall that way; no deliberate design. But every once in a while, coincidence rewards us. That was the ideal time to do it. It certainly seemed like a good omen. Her mom and dad were very devoted to one another. And it was a traditional wedding, even though I don't know if either one of us craved a big wedding, we were the first children in our two families to tie the knot. So it seemed to set the tone whether we meant it to or not. Suddenly we were role models, and everyone seemed to love it.

I had my brother Mike stand up for me as my best man, and there were four groomsmen, including Erik Tjaden and my longtime schoolmate Mike Rupe.

Susan had her bridesmaids, and I think we rented up every tuxedo in Southern Iowa at the time. Big congregation in the Christian Church; 300 people in attendance give or take...

RJA: *Would you do it again if you had to?*

Todd: I don't know. It's a very private issue, and even though I'm something of a showman at times, there are events like marriage that I feel deeply personal about. I know when my daughters Emily and Leah finally decide to get married, I will support their decisions in every way. But I keep trying to encourage them to elope. I would much rather spend the money sending them on a stellar honeymoon trip to some romantic far away place, so they can truly create some memories. Still, traditions are wonderful in their place.

RJA: *And at this point, you had the tradition going for you in the halls of academia and Indiana. So what were the last two years like for you?*

Todd: Frankly, it was the last two years where some of the most indelible transformations took place. I mean here I was working under (inarguably) one of the most influential chemistry professors in the country. I was, at this point, a teaching assistant in Synthetic Organic Chemistry, writing and conducting a thesis on homogeneous catalysis and carrying a grade point average between 3.8 and 4.0. I had just received a *Lubrizol Research Fellowship*

So things could not have been going better.

RJA: *Did you start to feel immortal at that point?*

Todd: You reach a point in your progress in the lab when you feel like you truly get a glimpse of how matter works, and for a brief time it imbues you with a sense of immortality. (For me it was probably my second year inside Ken Caulton's labs at IU.) It's pretty heady wine indeed, because for a flicker of time you think you've figured it all out. Then it quickly follows that reality bites and you come crashing down on the rocks with the realization that every new discovery you make will eventually fall by the wayside.

RJA: *I think it was Thomas Henry Huxley who said: "In the world of science, new ideas begin as heresy, advance into orthodoxy, and end as superstition."*

Todd: Dr. Huxley was pretty spot on. And the longer you work in a research environment the more humble you become. I mean the tapestry of discovery is so rich. Just when you think you're on top of it, there's always another challenge just outside the circle of your conclusions.

RJA: *How does that affect your sense of life? Did it tend to make you more agnostic or infuse you with a new sense of spiritual awareness?*

Todd: Well… yes on both counts. I think everyone in science hits that level where they feel what I call "a sense of arrogant atheism." I suppose I was no different...for about two months. Then the deeper you dive, the more you realize with all that happens in this universe there is unmistakably a Source.

RJA: *A Divine Source?*

Todd: Absolutely.

RJA: *I didn't mean to pull you off course. And that is a conversation I do want to take up later in our series. But for now let's get back to your timetable. I mean, here you are on a high career arc at Indiana. You're a kind of chemistry superstar—very high grade point average and you do your thesis on Synthetic Organic Chemistry. And you were pretty famous locally for your oral presentations of hypothetical platforms...and the skill with which you put them together.*

Todd: You've been studying...

RJA: *And you get something called the Nebergall Outstanding Inorganic Chemistry Research Award in 1991, and the Lubrizol Research Fellowship in 1991-1992. Sounds impressive. I'm sure they don't just hand those out to everybody.*

Todd: No it's pretty competitive. And The Nebergall Award for research in Inorganic Chemistry is an acknowledgement of your skill level and a very specific degree of achievement. The Lubrizol Fellowship is something you apply for. It is a very special research grant and award. But once again, they don't hand them out like candy. No question though, having them on my résumé did help line the path for my acceptance for a post doctoral position at the University of Utah in Salt Lake City.

RJA: *The Next Step on the Journey. What made you pick Utah?*

Todd: Several reasons really. Utah actually had one of the best programs for the research I was trying to accomplish, and I got a very coveted post-doctoral fellowship there. And I got to work under the aegis of Professor John Gladysz who was something of an academic legend.

It also happened to be one of the few universities in the country where Susan could get advanced certification as an MS CNM (board certified nurse-midwife). Virtually none of the Big Ten schools offered credits in the field of midwifery or even acknowledged it. And this was something she was very passionate about—that and her decision to go for her MS as a nurse practitioner…which she did.

RJA: *What was it like? That was quite a geographic cross-country jaunt of about 1500 miles or so. Was it a culture shock?*

Todd: Yes, but in so many good ways. Some of the best changes were social, but they tied directly back into my new position. As part of my post-doctoral program I was appointed to the university staff as an assistant in the Department of Chemistry there. So I was actually getting paid a living wage for what I was doing. A whopping $21,000 a year!

Next was the fact that for the first time either of us could remember, Susan and I actually had some free time on the weekends. So here we were, a couple of flatlanders from Iowa where the highest point of topography is a hilly cornfield, and suddenly we're surrounded by some incredible mountain ranges and several plush ski resorts like Park City, Deer Valley and Snowbird. The Wasatch Mountains are breathtaking. So we got involved in our share of skiing. And spending some weekends on the slopes was a lot of fun I can tell you.

But there wasn't just skiing. There were so many other things to do. There were those autumn weekends where we went to some University of Utah football games. (When you're in Iowa or Indiana or any Big Ten schools, tickets can be pretty hard to come by. But Utah's football program was pretty lousy at that time. So it was easy to get tickets.) And Salt Lake City was the most populous city we had ever lived in by far. So it was kind of a movable feast for a couple of years.

RJA: *...Which had to be great, because you finally had some breathing room.*

Todd: A little less time pressure. But by now you get my approach to things. The more I have in front of me, the more balls to juggle, the more fun I'm having.

RJA: *Actually I quite relate to that, which probably means we both need counseling.*

Todd: Ha ha! Or...maybe we're doing something right. I prefer to think the latter. And isn't it great?!

RJA: *OK. Now you were in your post-doctoral period at the University of Utah for just over two years, from 1992 to 1994. So what was your final point of focus under Dr. John Gladysz's program?*

Todd: John Gladysz was very well known for his work in chemical catalysis and chiral chemistry. What Dr. Gladysz somewhat famously did was help develop stereospecific chemistry using chiral metal complexes. In theory you could use these chiral metal complexes to make *enantiopure compounds* that provide a specific utility in drug development. (As an example: dopamine.) So he had the attention of major companies like Dow Chemical that ended up subsidizing much of his work.

RJA: *I think that might require a little translation for the layperson. I got the dopamine part at least. It has become a major component in many viable drugs used for the treatment of certain conditions.*

Todd: Well, the L-dopa form of it is. The "L" precursor is essential because L-dopamine is the stereoisomer that deflects light. And that's what allows it to pass the brain-blood barrier and be successfully absorbed into the system. And yes, L-dopamine in various forms has proven helpful in the reconfiguration of the brain's neurotransmitters in treating some pathologies—especially autoimmune conditions such as *Parkinson's disease* and more recently in eye deteriorations such as *macular degeneration*.

So, the work I was doing was developing a new kind of catalysis for small organic molecules to get this to the next level. I was also pretty good at translating this information, writing white papers on our findings and making oral presentations to summarize our data out of the Gladysz Research Group.

RJA: *That had to be a pretty valuable asset to any research group. You were kind of the mouthpiece for all the research. And you built quite a dossier on your ability to do so.*

Todd: That's kind of a retro way of putting it. But yes, I was honored to be a presenter for our group's findings when invited to do so. And doubtless this gave me some leverage when it came to getting the attention of major pharmaceuticals and chem-agra giants like Monsanto.

RJA: *Ah! Now we get to the next major paradigm shift in your life: The Monsanto period. I suppose that would take an entire chapter of its own.*

Todd: Oh, I think it does. But maybe we set some groundwork for it before we get there. So let's take a break and we'll pick it up from there.

Note: I notice one special thing about Todd Johnson, and that is his impeccable sense of timing. He knows just how far to push the envelope, and when to fold it down.

Todd, though confident and outgoing, never oversells his own story. There's always something left to find out. And you always end up wanting to know more. So we shut if off for now, and I know it to my bones that with the Monsanto years, the best is yet to come…

CHAPTER 4

MYTHS, MENTORS
AND MASTERS OF MOTIVATION

"Todd Johnson has great intuition about new ideas
and new concepts, plus the will to go out
and either prove or disprove his own hypothesis…
Then, once he commits to something,
he will do whatever it takes to make it succeed."

— Gary Mossman, Former CEO of CAMBREX

One thing you can't help but notice about Todd Johnson is his utter lack of grandeur. No gilded bedrooms or his name on every building this man, despite his relative renown, likes to keep things simple. If it didn't seem so effortless, I would suspect it was deliberate. Whatever the underlying motivation, Todd and Susan Johnson are very good about keeping their operation at Pomifera running just under the radar.

Their building is a modest 3500 square foot facility (plus another 5000 sq. ft. affiliation they use as a receiving and processing center). They have a small but efficient staff at both facilities and the only remnant of derring-do is a fire-engine red 2007

Chevy 2500 4 X 4 Heavy Duty Silverado that sits outside Todd's office about 12 hours day.

Yes, Todd drives what he refers to as a 10-year-old "truck" and—although he could afford just about anything at this point—he shows no indication of "putting on the dog."

By now, Todd and Susan have been both frugal and astute in their real-estate acquisitions. The Johnsons own several properties in a couple of states and just purchased forty choice acres in Southeastern Iowa in anticipation of expanding Pomifera at the appropriate time.

"It started as a habit, probably since graduate school, that we never live above our heads," Todd admits. "Now it's just a continuation of that lifestyle. And frankly I don't think it was as deliberate as it is a Midwestern custom. People out here aren't all that impressed with ostentation. And there's another philosophy behind it. From a professional aspect, people doing business at any level with Pomifera® will have the immediate awareness that we're all about keeping it real."

Since "keeping it real" seems like a good starting point for our next round of Q&A, I have to nail Todd down on a few personal points of view.

RJA: *I know we're due to launch off into the very exciting Monsanto chapter in your life, and I'm sure it will be quite a ride. But before we do, I'm taking you up on your suggestion that we cover a few points of personal philosophy before we get there. Why is that so important at this point?*

Todd: I think a good many stories fall apart because people tend to focus only on events—on what happens—when it's equally important if not more important to concentrate on why things happen and who the players are. That's the way you really connect the dots.

RJA: *So you'd like to dwell a bit more on subtext.*

Todd: ...Before we get back into "text." Yes I think that's a pretty good idea.

RJA: *OK. So I won't belabor the obvious. But you seem to play down your visibility in the community. To put it mildly you're not putting on airs. And you're very careful about how you grow. Do you think you're trying too hard to downplay your success?*

Todd: I don't think we're downplaying anything in a way. And the local community is very aware of our contributions. After all, by taking a junk fruit like hedge apples and turning them into a prolific commercial enterprise, we've employed about 15 people and added another $500 K to the local economy just to harvest and process the crops. So I think we've won some hearts and minds with that.

RJA: *Nevertheless, you're "keeping it real" as they say.*

Todd: Not to harp too much on the "rags to riches" thing, I do have to note that, when you come from modest beginnings, you automatically tend to be respectful of your success. You don't overextend yourself, and you're always mindful of what you achieve. In my experience, once you achieve something, you never want to grow complacent. I think if I have something that would ever keep me up at night it would be this: I'm desperately afraid of backsliding.

RJA: *But you don't strike me as someone who would ever let fear get the best of him.*

Todd: Well... fear is OK as long as it motivates you to accomplish something. As long as you keep it out on the periphery of your world, like a warning signal, it serves its purpose. Otherwise I'm very grounded. I know this much: I never want to be poor again. And I will do whatever it takes to provide for my family.

RJA: *So would you describe yourself as "driven?"*

Todd: I don't think there is any doubt about that. But I never drive out of control. I am, by nature, a risk taker. By the same token, I take calculated risks. I tend to be instinctive. I go with my gut. So by this time I've learned to trust my intuition, mainly because my judgment is almost always informed by my experience. I'm very deliberate about making a decision and living with that decision once I do. I'm also very comfortable about accepting the ideas of others. In fact, if there is one thing I've learned it is this: Recognizing a great idea and acting on it is every bit as important has having that idea in the first place.

Genius may be the mother of invention, but action is the midwife. You have to act on your intuition. Otherwise a great notion goes stillborn. Fortunately, I'm in a position to be able to act on my ideas. That's the beauty of being in charge of your own destiny.

RJA: *But you haven't always been in that position, have you? I mean you've had to navigate some pretty tricky layers of corporate, science and business "politics" (for lack of a better word). You've seen your share of intrigue, power-struggles, crises of corporate consciousness, and much more...*

Todd: I know! And hasn't it been exciting?! I think that's part of the crazy salad of going through any complex corporate, science or even academic structure. There's very often a great deal at stake—billions of dollars in some cases—and the closer you get to the source of power, the more treacherous the footing.

RJA: *And yet you have always seemed to do very well.*

Todd: Maybe so. If that's true—and I like to think it is—it's because I've had some pretty good mentors and teachers. Growing up, I had my father, my Uncle Don, and my coach Stan Huggins. Through my college years, I had some great professors who were stellar influences, captains of fate who helped steer my life decisions, and people who ended up being some really good friends. Lou Messerle was certainly the man who acted as my "spirit guide" to inspire and drive me up through the pathways of science, and specifically chemistry. And Dr. Ken Caulton was that paragon for me—who helped me re-form so many of my approaches to problem solving and how to just wring the most out of the cloth of my life.

RJA: *And you've paid them all—I think—sufficient tribute to this point. But what about your corporate life...and the people who helped you navigate the rather treacherous currents in that world? I'm sure there are some pivotal players in that arena as well.*

Todd: There's something I've noticed on the ladder to the top. (And it's definitely a ladder, and a careful step-by-step process, even though it may appear to be otherwise.) Anyway, that climb to the top comes about in two ways: First, the higher you go, the greater the game, the more the odds seem stacked against you. You are one of hundreds of candidates for Indiana's PhD program. You are one of 2000 for a corporate science position —virtually a small army of applicants—and yet you have no fear. At least I didn't, because there is that other element—that Positive Feedback Loop—working in your favor. You may call it the Law of Attraction, but it's essentially the same thing. Somehow it becomes a part of your evolution that you just learn how to win, and so all opposition peels away. And at the other end of it is that once-in-a-lifetime opportunity, and that mentor to help route you through it.

RJA: *So, you had two in the corporate world, I believe you mentioned. One is Mike Stern at Monsanto. And the other is Gary Mossman, a powerful influence who came later at CAMBREX I believe.*

Todd: That's correct. I think Mike was the biggest surprise for me, because he seemed to single me out of this absolute sea of applicants. There was this immediate kind of rapport—a sense of recognition I couldn't explain at the time. It's quite unusual because there are thousands of PhDs in the Monsanto culture, and somehow he singled me out.

Just as Ken Caulton helped refine the diamond in the rough in me, Mike Stern taught me how to be a functional scientist— and be *that guy*—who could make the translation of ideas from the lab to the product marketplace, from beakers to the boardroom. We were both Type-A personalities. So the intellectual connection was instantaneous.

As far as Gary Mossman is concerned, we had a great instant connection in that he liked my honesty. As head of a global drug manufacturing company like CAMBREX, he openly declared that he wanted answers, not lapdogs. I was able to provide him with real solutions to the questions that were raised. With Gary, you had to be responsible but forward-looking and be bold in your execution but realistic in your projections.

RJA: *I guess you'll want to explore a great deal more about both these gentlemen when we weave our way into the corporate scenarios. And I suppose it's more or less spiritual law that, once you are on purpose, the right person always seems to show up.*

Todd: By now, I'm convinced of it.

RJA: *So what do you look for in a mentor or teacher?*

Todd: The more I'm around and the more I take on in my life, the more I realize that everyone carries a bagful of wisdom if they'll just tap into it. And everyone you meet can teach you something. I know, especially when we live in that unique universe of science and the knowledge it unwraps, we hit that point when we think we've uncovered all the secrets of the universe. Then just as quickly you end up falling back into that final confession of Socrates: "As I come to the end of my life, I realize that I know nothing."

RJA: *Well, you're certainly not at the end of your life.*

Todd: I certainly hope not. Otherwise, I'd better ramp up my schedule.

RJA: *Still there have to be qualities that your major influencers (for lack of a better word) must have in common. Those who have had the most profound impact on your life and career—what do they have that sets them apart?*

Todd: Integrity certainly tops the list for me. All the women, being careful to include my mom, and men in my life—the ones I cherish most—have all been high character individuals. Then I would have to say that they are, without exception, people who possess qualities I may not have. I always look for people who challenge me, who make me reach and who bring a different kind of wisdom and knowhow into our relationship. As I said, if you open yourself up, everyone in life becomes your teacher. As for the Gurus, the major influences, they come less often. So you need to recognize them when you meet them.

Earlier you made reference to Napoleon Hill's concept of a "mastermind" group. And in a way that's the perfect concept. It's like a superstar Think Tank. The challenge with exceptionally gifted people is that they're always out there … doing! So it's very difficult to get them all in one place at one time. What we do end up doing is working with these magnificent souls at different stages in our lives. You take that leg of life's journey together, and you make every effort to pay it forward by making sure you give as much as you receive!

RJA: *Hence the true meaning of Synergy!*

Todd: "The whole is greater than the sum of its parts." Exactly.

RJA: *Anyone inspire you that you didn't know? Who have been the "great souls" in your life—the Einsteins, the Edisons, the DaVincis?*

Todd: Men of science usually have some kind of science hero as their "spirit guides," in some way. Louis Pasteur (the originator of Pasteurization) was that kind of person. But the man who inspired me the most had to be Nicola Tesla.

The things this man accomplished in one lifetime are almost otherworldly. Just the concept of the alternating current alone had to be the most revolutionary concept of our time. This was a man who in the first fifteen years of the twentieth century was able to drive cars and boats by remote control, and who actually conceivedd and designed a "cloud-busting" mechanism that could make rain. He even invented the prototype for the first torpedo, for heaven's sake!

This is the man who actually invented the wireless (radio) that Marconi took credit for. And his experimentation in nuclear technology was so advanced the government actually seized his files after he died (in 1943). Tesla was an inexhaustible genius, almost never slept and actually pushed himself beyond what we would acknowledge as physical limits.

That just scratches the surface of this man. He was the first man to delve into truly renewable energy sources. He designed and implemented the first ever Hydroelectric power plant (at Niagara Falls) where his works are now memorialized in the Tesla Museum. And I guess I could go on forever about the accomplishments that Tesla left as his legacy.

RJA: *An inspiration truly. And the Tesla car is now the first truly all electric luxury car. But what was it exactly that he did for you that made such an impact on your life?*

Todd: I think when I was in college, I caught fire because of the fact that this all came about through one man's genius as perhaps the greatest science mind of his time. And it was through studying his science disciplines that I truly believed I might be able to make a contribution.

RJA: *But he was never officially "credentialed" at the time. Neither were Edison or Einstein for that matter. They were all dropouts. Did you ever think of that? Kind of ironic, really.*

Todd: And it didn't take me long to realize that if any of these gentlemen were to try to advance their theories or hypotheses today, they might not even get to first base. Then again, they were Einstein, Edison and Tesla.

RJA: *But you're right. It might have been a great deal tougher. So we get back to the old issue of "the diploma." And by the time you move on to the next chapter in your life, you are loaded up with credentials. How did that make you feel?*

Todd: Buoyant. Humble. Ready to prove my mettle. You have to remember I had been training for this for nearly ten years. So for me it was "game on." I had a strong belief of purpose in my life. By then I had a sense of destiny and something of spiritual purpose.

RJA: *So…let's talk about "spirit" for a moment. I know that personal faith is always just that—deeply personal. And I know you've already expressed the belief that there are no atheists in foxholes…or laboratories.*

Todd: Well there are always some, I suppose. But I think it may be because they just haven't figured it out yet.

RJA: *You mentioned previously that the more you delve into causality in chemistry and science in general that there has to be an intelligent design behind all this.*

Todd: Even the term, intelligent design, has come under fire as a fundamentalist code word, when really it shouldn't be; because that's what it is. Of course, it's always a difficult path to travel down because matters of faith can be such flashpoints in any conversation. What is it they say, if you want to keep from alienating people you should never discuss religion or politics. And I've always thought that's cutting out some pretty good conversations. Although I do have to admit that, in today's climate, I tend to be aggressive in my avoidance of politics. At this point, no one I've ever seen in a political argument ever wins the debate. Opinions don't change, and friends too often get lost.

So, politics pretty much aside, what we like to do here is spend some of our lunch breaks with what people have come to call "Todd's Topics for Lunch." And the staff and I get into discussions about anything and everything. It's a kind of an open mike symposium where we all get to share our visions of life, movie reviews, art, science, book reviews, and even the principles and beliefs we hold most dear.

RJA: *I'd like to be a fly on the wall for some of those.*

Todd: Come and join us some time.

RJA: *So…religion comes up?*

Todd: Matters of faith come up. And I think that's where I've always drawn the line. Spirituality is an important journey. And I certainly believe in God and a divine source that guides all things of value. I was just never brought up in a religious family. Goodness knows we were imbued with a strong moral core. My dad always made sure we were honorable, polite and respectful young men and women. But we never had much formal religious training.

RJA: *But you are a man of faith.*

Todd: Yes, faith comes into everything I do. As a scientist you come to believe that there absolutely has to be a Creator. And the deeper you dive, the stronger your belief in that truth becomes. So, without actually verbalizing it on a daily basis you experience that serene sense of a Supreme Being guiding your actions. And it fills you with a sense of purpose that actually empowers you. So, yes! God directs everything I do. And that's what keeps my compass pointing North.

Now, am I going to be someone who goes out and proselytizes? No. But there is no question God exists. God's love exists. How you embrace it is entirely up to you. For me, I like to follow Abraham Lincoln's personal code when he said something like: "When I do good things, I feel good. When I do bad things, I feel bad…That is my religion."

So, since I have certainly learned right from wrong, I do as much good as I can. I help as many as I can. And I teach (and learn) whenever I can.

RJA: *So, when did your personal epiphany take place? Or was it any one thing? Often it's a series of events. So I sense that might have been it with you.*

Todd: It probably was. The first definitely came in the labs. When you behold the miracle of perfectly structured geometric elements as they recombine in infinite permutations, you just know there are Higher Hands at work. It's the only explanation.

The next true awakening came when I experienced the birth of our first child, Emily, and the miracle of that life coming into being. There is an awakening that takes place inside you that somehow defies explanation. And yet there it is. You have been witness to that miracle of creation, and you're never quite the same after that.

The third moment of great enlightenment for me came with in the hospice time Susan and I spent with her mother in her final days. We brought her home in her last few months to be with us. And the connection was something very special. Whether we intend it at this level of consciousness or not, there is a conversation that takes place about all things that are important. Sometimes it's even unspoken, but there is that sensibility to life after death—that there is a greater Source that awaits us once we leave this life.

RJA: *So how did all that affect you?*

Todd: With all these revelations, I think you tend to become existential in your decision-making. You grow more considerate of the long-range implications for everything you do. I think it also strengthens your moral core. And it has made me ever more aware of being a good role model for my children. I believe very strongly that the ultimate reflection of what we've done is in our children.

RJA: *And it appears that they have been a great source of pride.*

Todd: … And joy in my life! No question.

RJA: *And I note from your timetable that Emily's birth didn't come until you were already in the corporate world—at Monsanto, I believe.*

Todd: 1995. That's correct. By that time I had already waded waist deep into my first foray inside one of the most influential science and tech corporations in the world.

RJA: *By all evidence, it seems you were ready for what would come next. And didn't that chapter just seem almost magical in the way it all fell into place?*

Todd: A classic case of The Power of Intention…and to some degree an example of, "be careful what you wish for."

RJA: *Is this going to be a cautionary tale?*

Todd: More of a great adventure in all the right ways. Not without its hills and valleys, some power struggles, and many lessons

> *"Genius may be the mother of invention, but action is the midwife. You have to act on your intuition. Otherwise a great notion goes stillborn. Fortunately, I'm in a position to be able to act on my ideas. That's the beauty of being in charge of your own destiny."*

learned. But that's what makes the ride worth taking. And in this case it was quite a ride, and such a meaningful chapter in my life.

Note: At this point, I note that Todd Johnson has an unmistakable honesty of emotion that shows up in how he fixes his gaze. In every best sense of the word, his eyes betray him. When he is excited about something, or when the recollections please him, his eyes shine. And a kind of glow transforms his expression.

When he comes upon a difficult topic or something that goes against his standards, his features harden and his jaw tends to become square at the corners. In that respect he is very much a natural creature of God…and someone who has truly learned what really matters in life.

So, as we close this meeting, I can see that the next conversation is going to be one that both of us will enjoy as it unfolds.

CHAPTER 5

MONSANTO AND THE BUSINESS OF SCIENCE BREAKTHROUGHS

"We had hundreds of résumés for just one position. After I had them screened I still had about 100 sitting on my desk. Todd Johnson's just seemed to leap out of the pile at me. It turned out to be the only one I read…Then we did a phone interview and I knew he was the guy."

— Mike Stern, President and CEO, The Climate Corporation.

Indirectly I have Todd Johnson to thank for deciding to rethink my perspectives of some of the major Chem and Pharma conglomerates. And he did it with a simple truthful observation.

"Trust me. One misnomer about large chem-agra companies and the pharmaceuticals as well, is that they're opposed to 'natural' sources for their products. If there is a crop or a plant or a fruit in Nature that works to solve a problem, they'll be all over it. They just want what works."

Having been something of a corporate crusader and—with an advertising background—having borne witness to major "moral" corporations peddling what I considered to be immoral products, I have always kept my powder dry while taking aim on "profit motives" from some major marketers.

Todd helped put some of that skepticism to rest during our ensuing conversations. He also gave me a second pause for thought when he helped me break another bias.

"Companies like Monsanto and Pfizer spend tremendous amounts of money on research and development and testing of their new products. And very often they are groundbreaking. Those who wreck it for everyone are the middlemen—companies that come out with garbage knockoffs that promise the same benefit but end up doing more harm than good."

By now, Todd has earned my respect at several levels, not the least of which is the fact that he has created his own crossover dreams by going from a pure science background into finding "natural" products to help the human condition. The other one comes from the realization that he, more than anyone else, has the license to do so…literally! He has achieved his credentials. He has earned his spurs. He has he has mastered the Rule of Inference and by doing so has paved the way for us to follow.

Todd has a way of approaching a topic that causes one to sit up and take notice. That's because you know he has research and credibility on his side. I see it in him that much of this has to do with the fact that he was forged in the fire of corporate pressure that only a megalith like Monsanto can put in place.

Listening to his early recollections, many of which make it sound like a great adventure, I have to ask him why he didn't stay on and make it a career. His response makes it a great place to start the conversation.

RJA: *So, it sounds like the ultimate corporate adventure at Monsanto. And you seem to have been on a fast track to the top. What made you decide to move on?*

Todd: I'm sure it hit me later rather than sooner. But at some point I realized that I didn't want to be at any company where your final validation came with a gold watch and a pull date.

RJA: *So you didn't want someone else to be in control of your destiny. That, I believe, it's the classic response of a true entrepreneur.*

Todd: …To which I plead guilty on all counts! Yes, I did absolutely recognize that I wanted to have my hand on the wheel of my own ship of state. In the final analysis, that's the only thing that made sense.

RJA: *But I don't believe you were that way at first. As I recall you were very excited about your first major encounter with the corporate culture and the Magical Mystery Tour that turned out to be what I would have to call "the business end of science."*

Todd: Good way of putting it. Because that's what Monsanto was all about. They loved science as long as it translated into some useful purpose in the marketplace. And I'm sure that is still a part of their culture even now.

RJA: *So…let's backtrack a bit in time to that point at the University of Utah when you had become something of an academic superstar already loaded with credentials and known for writing white papers that were becoming works of academic legend.*

Todd: That maybe laying it on a little thick. But OK, I was feeling pretty good about things. And I did have a sense that something very special was just around the corner.

RJA: *And that was Monsanto...*

Todd: I had some feelers out. But Monsanto was definitely my first choice. They just had so much going for them. And they honored chemistry as a profession. I think some of their founders had chemistry backgrounds and that philosophy of respect for serious science still reflects in everything they do.

RJA: *So you were among a pretty elite group petitioning for a position there. Even so, didn't you tell me there were more than 2000 applicants for the same position, and only two slots available?*

Todd: Closer to 2500 applicants in the beginning, so I was told. Then they narrowed it down. And yes, only two us out of that very prestigious field were actually awarded a research position. Remember these were all PhDs in the field of applied and synthetic chemistry. So when you get picked out of that bunch, you are definitely at the top of the food chain. I mean here you have a Fortune 200 Company with annual revenues of $14 billion and about 20,000 employees worldwide. And here I was coming into their Corporate Research Division, hand picked by one of their rising stars, to be a research specialist in his very influential branch. I mean, as I found out quickly, that was the place to be.

RJA: *So, your job description was something like overseeing, "the development of homogenous catalysts in oxidation, carboxylation, and carbonylation to be utilized in the manufacture of amino acids* *for specified product lines and new products," or something like that. That's quite a mouthful. Can you translate for those of us less erudite than your average Mensa PhD?*

Todd: Yeah, well I can. And then I'll probably have to translate the translation. But that's OK too, because that more or less defines what I had to do at Monsanto. My job was primarily to make business and marketing sense out of what we came up with in the labs. At least that's what it evolved into. What I ultimately did was lead a research group that developed and patented an environmentally benign amino acid program that was a true commercial attempt at achieving a zero carbon footprint!

RJA: *So, that's a good thing? Right?*

Todd: Well, most if not all of what we attempted to do was driven to the general good. When you get down to it, scientists are guided to operate by the same Hippocratic oath as MDs or anyone else in the healing arts: "First do no harm." Granted sometimes you have to go through harmful steps in the lab, missteps and occasional out-and-out calamities. But that too is all in the job description. Along the way, the main thing about what we did was to focus entirely upon showing the people at corporate that something could actually be made into a product that would become a broad-spectrum benefit—either in industry, agriculture or the ultimate consumer.

RJA: *Which marketplace?*

Todd: There are about ten when you get down to it.

RJA: *And that job apparently fell to you. Or so I understand. I believe you were in charge of what…eight to ten MS and PhDs in Chemistry and chemical engineers?*

Todd: Something close to that at the end of my tenure at Monsanto. Just me in the beginning. We had a couple of Bachelors of Science thrown in for balance. At any rate, it was kind of a think tank task-force environment combined with a pressure cooker because we were constantly called on to produce results. In fact we were pretty much required to issue monthly reports and make oral presentations so we could get sector funding for our projects. And that always took some doing.

RJA: *In what ways?*

Todd: Whatever our test initiatives in the labs, they had to be drawn toward a goal. And we had to set up milestones and markers along the way, and then articulate them to the "big boys" at the top of the Division—one step below the boardroom.

RJA: *A strong suit of yours, I believe. Weren't you noted for your white papers and your ability to articulate them in some kind of public forum?*

Todd: Sort of a career pattern I had set in my post-doctoral papers. I guess so. Somewhere in my six years of graduate studies, I had just sort of figured it out. White Papers require a certain level of detachment, and an ability to see all aspects of an issue in hopes of finding a model that works.

So it comes in with a kind of healthy skepticism and emerges with conclusions that you hope will offer some "warts and all" optimism for what you've been tasked to do. And if you're a guy who can design catalysts in reaction chemistry and make the translation successfully to a useful product platform, you get to be pretty much in demand.

Anyway, one thing we learned to do was cut our losses quickly. If we found a platform that wasn't working, we scrapped it as soon as the conclusions became evident…and just moved on to the next big thing.

RJA: *…And you were more or less handpicked to head this group up almost out of the gate, or so I understand. I believe Mike Stern saw that leadership quality in you early on, because when I talked with him, he pointed up the fact that anytime he had a really tough project, you were the one to volunteer to take it on. And you apparently did it 100% of the time. I think Mike said, "Todd had that rare talent and intellect to see the end result of something, plus the raw drive to just get it done no matter what." Quite a compliment.*

Todd: I'm certainly honored that Mike placed that kind of trust in me. And I confess to the fact that I welcome pressure. In fact I love pressure. The tougher the task, the greater the high you're going to have once you've mastered it. Some people, I suppose, are drug addicts and alcoholics. My addiction—my only addiction ever—would have to be the adrenalin rush I get from pressure situations.

RJA: *I guess that's what Mike Stern saw in you. Because he was your immediate supervisor and he seemed to put you at the head of things right away.*

Todd: Mike Stern and I connected instantly, from day one. He was that guy you see who just has "winner" written all over him. He was about seven years older than I, and anyone with eyes could see that Monsanto corporate had already tapped him for a major role in their future plans. Mike was Technology Director at Monsanto Research when he put me in front of this task force. And he did more than anyone to teach me the ropes, and the step-by-step milestones and markers we needed to get things done. He was also a passed master at navigating the corridors of power at corporate. So he was very good at helping me develop the people skills to team-build inside my own group—to make others feel a valuable part of the process.

Granted, I had tapped the brakes on my bulldozer approach to everything and everyone by the time I'd gotten out of grad-school. But I still had that compulsive drive that I think—without any real intention on my part—tended to intimidate others. Mike showed me how to smooth out my approach to team building and making others feel valuable to the process. For lack of a better description, he taught me how to "empower others to feel they had made a contribution," and it certainly paid dividends for me during the rest of my career.

RJA: *So, let me paint the picture if I may: You're in this very influential agrochemical biomedical giant corporation with offices in 14 countries and 20,000 employees, about 8% of which were PhDs. And here you were right in the middle of Monsanto Chemical Research and head of what amounted to an* R&D *Swat Team.*

Todd: It was something of a summit position in Monsanto Chemical Research: the ultimate status symbol. It was the Think

Tank of Monsanto. Rubber, chemical, pharmaceutical, agricultural divisions—all allocated headcount and supplies to us.

We were there to solve problems, issues or chemical conundrums with complete impunity and with an eye on optimum output while getting manufacturing costs down.

We were virtually science-to-market converters without limits. We did all this stuff the research chemists didn't get, because we knew how to make it feasible, tangible and marketable. And Mike had helped me master the system of *variable design*—meaning you took into account all variable design options for any project, product or formula, culled the losers and proceeded from there to the best possible solution.

RJA: *Sounds pretty foolproof. Was it?*

Todd: Nothing in science and technology is fool proof. But it did enable us to cut our losses quickly and come up with more right solutions in a shorter period of time.

RJA: *Was it that high pressure all the time? That can really fry you after a while.*

Todd: Not all the time, but certainly most of the time. But it was all worth it. Whatever our challenges, whatever the pressure, Monsanto Chemical Research was the place you wanted to be. That was Mike Stern's personal duchy, and I had just been knighted. We would bust our buns, put our best proposals forward and... if your Technology Director (Mike in this case) supported your findings, and if the division liked it, they would fund you for the year. So we virtually had carte blanche for some projects.

It was highly competitive and in all the good ways a "take no prisoners" atmosphere. People who made the most impact got hotshot status, deep pocket funding, and rapid advancement to bigger and better things. For us it was truly the Best of the Best—the corporate version of Top Gun.

RJA: *And you were kind of the Recruitment Poster Triple Ace for the group. From what I understand you got to use your presentation skills quite often.*

Todd: I've always been blessed with my share of good presentation skills. I had gained something of reputation for defining my group's findings and translating them into readable conclusions. And since I wasn't the least bit shy about presenting them in person, I got to travel to some pretty interesting places in the world, stand in front of some very large groups inside the Monsanto culture, and present our findings. In a small way, I got to taste some sampling of celebrity. At least our work was being celebrated.

RJA: *A pretty glamorous portrayal. But surely there had to be some occasional dodgy corporate politics along the way.*

Todd: That's always the wild card in megalithic corporations.

RJA: *Did they ever get in the way?*

Todd: Unless you're very lucky it's inevitable. But that's part of the Rubix of high profile undertakings of any kind. And the higher the stakes the greater your chances of getting on a collision course of ideologies. The good news is that I was on such a roll for the first two years I was there that I managed not to get caught up in it, which was very lucky for me.

RJA: *What was it about that period in your career that made it so special? Can you describe it for me?*

Todd: Thanks to Mike Stern's guidance and mentoring, and I guess due to my workaholic approach to being the best at what we did, I got onto a very fast track. The more successes we had in the labs—the better the translation I was able to make to present "street smart" product technology—the more responsibility I was given and the (stated or unstated) power that went with it. Within a couple of years, I went from being on my own and my lab group to having more than a dozen chemists and engineers reporting to me.

Being Mike Stern's, "ace in the hole," certainly helped give me some cachet inside Monsanto corporate. And before long I was working to create what they call the Redbook inside Monsanto—a code key that defines the science procedural "matrix" for all successful projects.

By year two and three I had achieved what they call the "Monsanto Reach Award" for outstanding product creation and development. And I had some patents going-in with my name on them. In a way, I was a "Technical Group Leader," but without the title.

By that time, Mike Stern was on a fast track to what they call the C-Level Street, and I was right there with him. I had become a "valued researcher" inside the Monsanto corporate culture and was getting quite a bit of notice on my own.

And for at least the first two years, I was enjoying being "that guy." And once you get to be *that guy* inside the corporate power structure, you really get to enjoy the fruit of your labors. You're given immediate access to something they call "Christ" outings.

And those included special perks, holidays, golf weekends and ski-trips. It was something very special.

RJA: *And you're a scratch golfer, I understand.*

Todd: Not anymore, but I was pretty good in my day. It may be my favorite sport because it's just you and the course, your nerves and your will against the forces of nature—no place to hide. It's the ultimate pressure game.

RJA: *…Which is obviously the way you like it. What about your private life at that time? You were on what seemed like a high-speed rail to the Promised Land.*

Todd: Couldn't have been better. We were living in O'Fallon, Missouri, a sort of up and coming suburb of St. Louis Metro Area at that time. Susan was running a clinic for St. Charles County. The money was great and getting better, because we got rapid advancement, performance bonuses, and the men at the top of the Division were starting to take notice. We were on that positive feedback loop that seems to go on unbroken for quite some time. Then we had an additional blessing in 1995 with the birth of our first daughter Emily. And what a truly life-changing experience that was.

RJA: *That was right in the middle of your second year with Monsanto. That had to be a game change.*

Todd: Very much so…and in all the most positive ways. I mean, you think you're life has a very special purpose, and then that other part of your love that completes the family cycle comes into fill your days, and it changes you. So I became even more driven to succeed. At that point, I had a whole new level of motivation; not that I really needed one.

RJA: *So all this was going on while you are at the peak of your game? That's a lot to juggle.*

Todd: A real pressure cooker but a great place to be. I mean, my group had no boundaries. We were the paradigm shifters (if that term exists). We challenged and overcame issues that academic research chemists just didn't get. It was so much a performance-based paradigm. If you delivered the goods, you were promoted and awarded with more funds. It was a great place to be.

RJA: *A good many huge corporations like that can get a bit parochial. Sometimes they get bogged down in the politics of seniority. You mean that didn't happen here?*

Todd: Seniority didn't count for much at Monsanto in those days. Especially in the mid 1990s when I was there, they were virtually a meritocracy. They rewarded outstanding performance above all else. And Mike Stern always had my back. I mean he made sure I got the recognition I deserved. And one thing you have to remember at a high-profile international mega-corp like this, in terms of education and credentials, virtually *everyone* was your peer. In some ways you felt like you were being cloned. But you also enjoyed that comfort zone where you find yourself in some very lofty intellectual company. So no one had to be dragged along to accomplish the goals you'd set before you. In fact, the corporate culture wouldn't stand for it.

So, to draw a sports metaphor, it was like a Major League franchise, and I was enjoying the status of an emerging superstar on the team.

RJA: *It would seem like the ideal place to go the distance.*

Todd: On the surface anyway…and some people did. Mike is still there, as CEO of one of Monsanto's divisions. So it was definitely a path to take if you're driven that way. I wasn't.

RJA: *So you took the road less traveled…which means at some point you arrived at a point of critical mass in your thinking. ("Critical mass," by definition, being the point at which change occurs.) So when did that time come for you?*

Todd: I suppose it came in stages. And I had hints of it as early as 1996. Nonetheless, I continued to perform and get awards for my work and patents that continued to be credited to me. So the perks and the prestige were certainly issues that imbued one with a sense of security and even the illusion of longevity.

In 1996, I had won my first Monsanto Reach Award, which was something the company did to acknowledge outstanding achievement in new product development and groundbreaking discoveries. Inside Monsanto Corporate Research this was the equivalent of winning an Oscar or an Emmy.

RJA: *…Something you won two years running, in 1996 and 1997, I believe.*

Todd: Understand this was back in a decade when Monsanto itself was enjoying all kinds of positive public perception. In fact it won the *Forbes Magazine* Award as one of the Top Ten Most Innovative companies in America. They won it three times in the 1990s and (ironically) in 2017 for their new "Analytics Platforms." So I have to guess that they're still doing some things the right way.

RJA: *This all sounds perfect, and yet something or some set of events set off a shift in your thinking. I mean all this fast track, career spike and exit happened in about 4 ½ years. So what changed?*

Todd: The corporate philosophy underwent a tectonic shift that shook the whole infrastructure. It started in 1997, and it continued gradually but relentlessly for the next couple of years. They started selling off pieces of Monsanto bit-by-bit, lopping off divisions, merging others. New players and a new culture started to subsume what I felt had been highly synergistic work environment. They were really taking out and retiring upper mid-level management. (So much for the pension plan and the "gold watch" culture.) And even though they treated me well—and even though Mike Stern counseled me to ride out the storm—I lost whatever illusions I might have had about retiring after a long career ride at one company.

By that time, I had certainly seen all the warning signs.

RJA: *What warning signs?*

Todd: It was obvious they were applying their own strange version of *affirmative action* inside the divisions and even inside their "core research groups." Part of that turned out to be setting traps to run off tenured mid-level people without paying them the retirement packages to which they were entitled.

On a personal level, I went from enjoying the status of an award winning high-profile wunderkind in Monsanto Chemical Research (MCR) to being "randomly" drug tested as much as six times in 12 months—and for no apparent reason other than the fact that this was the new mindset that had taken over.

I have to admit that at the time I found it highly amusing since I've never taken anything much stronger than aspirin in my life. But there they were literally trying to nail key employees in what, by all appearances, seemed to be a corporate witch-hunt. Not exactly something designed to build *esprit de corps*. And it cost them in the long run. So I started entertaining other offers, and one just jumped out at me.

By that time, I also realized that I was not meant to breed in captivity. At some point I was going to have to be lord of the jungle—my jungle. So even then the heed and cry of the entrepreneur was echoing in my ears.

RJA: *Did they make any effort to keep you there at Monsanto? I mean, surely you had proved your worth.*

Todd: Yes, they absolutely did. In fact they made me an offer that included 50% raise in salary to stay on. But by that time, my trust level had been shaken more than a little. Imagine, if you will, the fact that you have formed a seemingly invincible team, a family of sorts, and you are hitting winner after winner. And you're the shining lights of a corporation. Then you wake up one day, and some of your key people have either left or been laid off. And suddenly you've become a "stranger in a strange land." Nothing seems as it was before.

So it was time to make my move.

My sister Leah and I love to tease our dad to keep him grounded. And yet in all the ways that matter Todd Johnson is the best role model anyone could ever want. He is a very modest fellow, and yet once he decides to take something on, he never, ever gives up.

~ Emily Johnson

RJA: *The end of an era.*

Todd: So to speak. But it was time. No regrets. I have a bushel barrel of great memories from my time there. Some invaluable lessons learned, I sustained a faith in my ability to take on any challenge and win: to know that you could thrive in "the show"; to prove that a kid from small town Iowa did succeed in ways that no one in Bloomfield could ever imagine; to know that the Big Ten can intellectually take on the Ivy League and come out on top; and finally to co-create some wonderful friendships in the bargain.

RJA: *So what were the next steps for you? You went from Monsanto—a $14 Billion industry Leviathan—to a company called ABC Laboratories.*

Todd: Right! A company of 250 employees and about $13 million in annual revenues perched on the very edge of extinction.

RJA: *"A Target for Elimination" that you helped rescue, by all available evidence.*

Todd: Well… as they say in the world of relationships, "It's complicated."

RJA: *But fun, for you apparently. You did some pretty remarkable things while you were there.*

Todd: Always leave things better than you found them, I hope. And that will make a terrific opening gambit for our next chapter…

CHAPTER 6

CHANGING LANES

Todd and Susan bought this classic historical house in Boonville,
Missouri. It was beautiful and huge but was in need of repairs, and
perfect for a renovation "flip." It was set in kind of a sketchy neigh-
borhood. So sketchy, in fact, that some gang bangers used to cruise
up and down the block on a daily basis…One day Todd had put up
with enough. So he goes out into his front yard with a baseball bat
in hand to confront them and announced with that edgy confidence
of his: "You will no longer come onto my street." The gang bangers
blew out of there and never came back again.

— Eric Neuffer/Former VP of Business Development,
CAMBREX

There is an unwritten rule of business in the New Millennium: *For the gifted, mobility equals success.* Seemingly, it slams up against all the tenets of corporate logic since the beginning of time. Back in the day, it was a common perception that anyone employed by a major corporation in virtually any industry was been given the keys to the Kingdom. Stability, job security, steady advancement, a pension plan, retirement with honors—all these things and more seemed to come with the passage.

Then, in the early 1990s, there was a tectonic shift that took place. Loyalty, tenure and planned careers—all became fodder in a new attrition of Darwinian economics that seemed to subsume the soul of many global corporations. An entire generation of mid-level executives, especially those of a certain age, found themselves shot down in a fusillade of cutbacks. Leveraged out of their careers a good ten years before retirement, many of them were forced to reboot a career with limited options.

A new incarnation of corporate cultures suddenly found them expendable. Bolstered by relentless cost accounting and the onslaught of computerization, entire professions were obliterated. And, as so often happens, the bottom line started looking so fat that suddenly no one was safe.

Suddenly a legion of lost executives started flooding the market. And soon there would be a manpower glut—unless you were smart and very, very agile.

Todd Johnson had seen it coming all along.

"I don't think I was the only one who did," Todd admits. "And it really didn't take a rocket scientist (or a PhD in Chemistry) to read the 'Hieroglyphics of the New Success.' The bottom line, especially in the new dynamic of high profile companies like Monsanto, was that it was every man for himself."

Todd uses that for his opening comment in our next set of conversations. And as usual, he has something of a sixth sense about where left off last time (last chapter) and where we need to pick up. I can tell by the somewhat mischievous look that Todd is giving me that this is going to be a fun ride—something akin to a bullet train into an undiscovered country.

That new planet, that hidden land, has always held a fascination for me, because although it appears on the surface to be nuts and bolts and pedestrian to the average consumer, this hidden realm of science and technology is the actual wheelhouse where the fine tuning of all progress takes place. The L-dopa that ameliorates Parkinson's disease, API's (Application Program Interfaces) that build tools for software applications, the healthy growth media that create insect resistant grow-crops that reproduce at quadruple their former levels to feed a hungry world—all these things and more are dreamt of, developed and given birth here. So even brushing up against this "dull world" of shining ideas instills me with a sense of both appreciation and awe.

And so we begin…

RJA: *So…we've now arrived that critical juncture where Todd Johnson is in his mid-thirties, and has achieved a certain level of celebrity in the world of advanced science and chemical research.*

Todd: Almost sounds like a contradiction in terms. Doesn't it?

RJA: *Well, by all appearances, it was anything but dull. Starting in 1999, you worked for about five companies (including your own). And according to your CV you went through three of them at least twice.*

Todd: Yeah. No one could ever accuse me of burning bridges.

RJA: *Rather unusual. And it seems on the surface to fly in the face of every cliché I've ever heard about science nerds and job security. But at this point, I've been made aware of the fact that you are not a pure science nerd. You are that rather remarkable hybrid who becomes the*

Messenger between two worlds—translating the intricate value of one to the other—that turns out to be its own special niche.

Todd: Or perhaps the absence of one. I like to think my greatest strength is breaking patterns—and not being able to be pegged because of it.

RJA: *Applying the Law of Disruption?*

Todd: An overrated term if there ever was one. I know it's been quite the buzzword for the last five years or so. But it's more of an escape word to me. It implies something like the upside of chaos. And I'm a firm believer that success is series of steps. You may get bumped against the rails on the way to pursuing it, but you never lose sight of your objectives.

RJA: *Did you? Even for a little bit? I mean, here you are a science rockstar with Monsanto one day and the next you're taking over a science division in a company perched on the very precipice of disaster: ABC Laboratories, wasn't it?*

Todd: Well you have to admit, I've never been one to dodge a good challenge.

RJA: *So you go from a Fortune 200 company with 20 thousand employees and annual revenues of $15 billion (give or take), and here you end up as Director of Operations at a contract research company with a staff of 25 and annual revenues of a little more than $2.5 million. Wow! Talk about culture shock!*

Todd: I know. Trust me. No one was more surprised than I was. But it was the only option available to me at the time. Because part of my game plan for leaving Monsanto was to find a position with a company that would help me help Susan fulfill her dream. After all, she had done so much over the years to help me get to where I was—with a PhD and a prestige job at Monsanto—it was time for me to pay it forward… and back to her.

RJA: *So how did that happen? Sounds like some pretty tricky waters to navigate.*

Todd: It was and it wasn't. As it turned out, as part of her new level achievement with her MS as a nurse practitioner and her Certified Nurse Midwifery degree, she had been offered a faculty position at the University of Missouri in Columbia. It was such a career coup for her at a Big 12 University and the dream job she'd always wanted, I thought this would be a good time for me to take yet another leap of faith.

So even though Monsanto had made me this pretty phenomenal offer, I literally sent in a flyer and a cover letter to this small contract research organization in the space of Analytical Biochemistry.

RJA: *A pretty good space to work in at the time. I mean that's where some things were really happening.*

Todd: You may know that. And I may know that, but I'm not sure they did. Anyway, it turned out to be a pretty good deal for them—at least they recognized it as such—because they brought me on board a few days after I applied as their Director of Operations for the pharmaceutical and radiopharmaceutical business unit.

RJA: *One that sounds like it was something for which you were possibly overqualified.*

Todd: Overqualified in one area, perhaps underqualified in another. I certainly knew the area of Chemistry, Biotechnology and commercial scale-up. But I certainly had a learning curve when it came to establishing and navigating GMP systems and jumping through hoops with the FDA.

RJA: *GMP? Good Manufacturing Practices?*

Todd: Correct. It was an entirely new space for me, and one for which I had not been trained. But I had the FDA's Policies and Procedures Manual and some colleagues willing to teach. So learning to navigate this was just a matter of study and application.

Whatever I was originally brought in to do, it was definitely a hybrid position. Technically my title was something bizarre like Head of Synthesis, which was a euphemism for the fact that I was responsible for transforming the future of the company into a quality driven organization. More than that I was the guy who had to make things profitable.

RJA: *Still, you leapt into the breach to do this. Gutsy, I have to say.*

Todd: And risky as it turns out, because ABC Laboratories were not in very good shape when I got there. In the first place, I had taken on something of a pay cut to be there. It was about

20% less than Monsanto's generous offer to me to stay, but just enough of a decent paycheck for me to continue with my career while Susan was able to reach the top of the mark in hers.

What I didn't know and couldn't have anticipated was the fact that ABC was running red ink. My "GMP Business Unit" was only on an annual run rate of about $150 K. The company as a whole was only generating $12-13 million dollars a year. Of course context is everything. So, due to the fact that there were about 200 employees, productivity as I found it was extremely low.

RJA: *Which means very little profit and free cash flow after all costs and salaries are paid.*

Todd: Correct. So in the beginning at least, there were those times of the month when we all had concerns over whether or not our paychecks would even clear. It wasn't that they were broke as such. It was that the chain of cash flow was weak to the point of being anemic. To spice the sauce a bit further, I soon came to realize that I had been put charge of a Science Division whose VP and Head of Research was totally convinced that business and marketing were the enemy.

And since it was my job to help convert their research findings into a viable product for the marketplace, it was my primary responsibility to bring revenues into the house.

That meant I had to create a pitch book and get questions you couldn't answer from sources no one dared tap. I had to create an ABC survival model for my business unit, and then go out and sell the business.

RJA: *So, it sounds like the entire weight of ABC had been placed on your broad shoulders.*

Todd: More or less. Compound that by the fact that ABC's Research Director, in charge of their analytical program, was totally intimidated by me. Although it was 180 degrees away from my intention, I think he was terrified that I'd been brought in to replace him. Compound that with his innate dread of the marketing end of the business, and he managed to dig in his heels every time some inroads were made to build out capabilities and transform the unit into a quality organization.

So there you had it. Like it or not, I was fighting a battle on two fronts just to generate a platform for ABC to simultaneously survive and thrive into the world of contract drug development.

RJA: *Well…in a situation like that, it seems to me that it was about time to apply a tactic from Sun Tzu's* The Art of War—*"When confronting two enemies, it is always best to attack and defeat the weakest one first."*

Todd: Well, Sun Tzu was a wise man, and at some level I must have tapped into his strategy tables, because that is precisely what I did. First I went into my supervisor the CEO of the company and issued an ultimatum that either this head of research answer my timetables and product/quality responsibility models or I would resign, and they could reboot with someone else.

RJA: *Apparently it worked. You got what you wanted. You stayed and apparently flourished…at least the company did.*

Todd: It didn't happen overnight, but it happened pretty quickly. And frankly in the shape we were in when I got there, we had nowhere to go but up. The computers were antiquated. Much of the research staff were completely unqualified to be in that department. So I had to fire about one-third of them and train the rest to learn how to work with the protocols set by both Big Pharma and the FDA.

Once you get in the door with Big Pharma they'll give you an insight into their way of doing business, including glimpses of their expectations of quality. The FDA is pretty straight ahead, and they're clear about their caveats and ladders of approval. And believe me, groups like Pfizer and Merck are even more item specific, and none of them are going to even let you in the door until you pass their quality audits.

What's more, we had some pretty big-gun pharmaceutical companies in our sights as possible clients. So for me, that meant building the team that could do that. Many had the wrong skill-set. Others had absolutely zero capacity for problem solving. And once I'd culled that group out, I had to groom somebody who could become a leader inside our group.

RJA: *I'm guessing that by then you had already "sussed" somebody out.*

Todd: I did. But I'd almost lost him before I promoted him. He was a research scientist named John Bucksath. And from the very beginning he was a leader of the disaffected. He made his concerns known upfront and was highly vocal in his criticism of the way things had been run – especially with respect to the proper way to build an audit proof quality-driven laboratory. On the surface he might have appeared to be perpetual malcontent. But at least he had the balls to express himself out in the open. And every time he brought up an issue, I couldn't help but notice that every observation he made was spot-on correct.

Someone else might have looked at him as a troublemaker. But when I took a closer look I realized that he was one of the few people under my banner who actually knew what the heck was going on.

You see, pretty early on I had been told by the CEO to fire John. My immediate response to the CEO was that there was going to be a lot of things that I would do at ABC, but one of them that I wouldn't do was fire John Bucksath!

After a few months, I called him into my office to tell him so. And I think when I did he was pretty certain he was going to be fired. John was a gentle giant who stood about 6'7". He was really a wonderful guy once you cut through all the professional frustration at work. And I think he actually sat back down in the chair when I told him that I respected his work—and that rather than fire him I was actually going to give him a promotion.

Fast-forward to 2004-2005 when I returned to ABC. And behold: John Bucksath had become the President of the GMP business unit we had built together from ground zero. It was without a doubt the most profitable business unit in the company and the driver for all things at ABC. John ultimately became the CEO of the company and guided it through a merger which ultimately created liquidity and value for all ABC shareholders. So I guess I turned out to be a pretty good judge of talent.

RJA: *Speaking of talent, didn't you also manage to convince Erik Tjaden to join you there at ABC before you left?*

Todd: That's right I did. Erik had a pretty plumb research position at Union Carbide, and I did manage to entice him over with a rather perfect position working with me, with the possible notion of his replacing me—if/when. He came aboard in March of 2000 and by May of that same year, I was gone.

RJA: *Did he object to your doing that and then almost immediately moving on?*

Todd: Not really. Mobility was the game at that time. In the world of chemistry, research and marketing, you had to be fast on your feet. You had to be willing to move and make changes, and everybody got that. Besides, Erik was always someone who could handle himself in any situation. He had the chops, and we both knew it. So we always used that wonderful mental shorthand between us to just get on with it whenever the time was right. I also immediately became his biggest customer when I went to work for my new employer MetaPhore Pharmaceuticals, Inc.

RJA: *Meanwhile you had quite a two-year run at ABC. You built up a winning team. You garnered a superb reputation for yourself and, I believe, helped bolster ABC's GMP business unit revenues up 8 to 10 fold from 1998 to 2000.*

Todd: Right, well it takes about 18 months to get from the laboratory to any kind of developed product. When I got there, ABC was having trouble making a two-year turnaround. They were locked in research dead-ends that didn't go anywhere. What I was able to do was teach them how to cut their losses and get on a viable product and quality path that worked.

What happened finally was that John and I got them signed as the lead GMP analytical lab for an unknown but up-and-coming megacorp Sepracor™. ABC ultimately landed the lion's share of the FDA registration work on a monster drug product called Lunesta®—a formulation that later became a multibillion-dollar product. I think anyone alive in the first part of the 21st Century saw that strange luminescing butterfly sleep-aid commercial.

And inside the two years I was there we got their revenues up to a growing and profitable run rate that evolved into a company that grew very quickly to $20-25 million per year.

RJA: *Mission accomplished. So meanwhile, you made all these contacts on behalf of ABC. You seem to have enhanced your industry cachet even further. While you're building this business unit from ground zero, your star continues to rise. And you get an offer from a very well funded start-up pharmaceutical company, Metaphore, headed up by a former associate from Monsanto.*

Todd: One of the side-benefits of being the interface expert at ABC, and more or less the face of the drug development franchise, also meant that I was able to network with some pretty influential people and companies! So yes that all worked in my favor. This especially played into the fact that I knew the new CEO at Metaphore, Dennis Forester and his VP of R&D Dennis Riley, because Dr. Riley (DR) had been a peer of Mike Stern's at Monsanto. And we knew each other from there.

Dennis Riley had known about my track-record at Monsanto and had placed some critical early work with me at ABC. That meant he had a very good idea of what I could so. And after two years, I was at least able to cycle out of ABC and into an even more challenging position as Metaphore's Director of Development.

RJA: *...which is definitely an adventure all its own. We'll cover that in a moment. But before we do, let me ask you about your personal life at the time. You were obviously working long hard hours. Susan had her faculty position at the University of Missouri. Your daughter Emily was about three at the time you moved. So did you actually find time to have a life outside of business?*

Todd: Well, we actually managed to do so rather nicely, and in a couple of very important ways. First we found this phenomenal historical home outside of Columbia that was a classic kind of Mediterranean Mansion—brick to the core of its foundation and replete with high floor-to-ceiling cantilever windows. It was definitely a fixer-upper in a fairly sketchy neighborhood. So Susan and I got it at a price. But in all sorts of ways it was like finding buried treasure. Because it had some really classic appointments—like rich interiors, tile floorings and classic hardwood floors. Still it was in dire need of repair. But we knew that every effort we put in would increase the value of the home. So we were always spending time and elbow-grease upping its appearance, finding ways to redo the interior room-by-room as we went. So it was kind of a full time project, making it beautiful and knowing all the while that every bit of reworking we did was helping to increase its value.

It may have seemed to be a drudge, but it was also a great deal of fun. And we both got to hone our creative skills in carpentry, painting and interior design.

RJA: *Seems like a lot of hard work on top of all that hard work. Was that really something you wanted to take on?*

Todd: Well let me give you a little backstory leading up to it, because before that we had this house in Columbia, MO that was virtually eating us alive. It was a mansion but in every sense of the word came at a price. It was 5 bedrooms 4 ½ baths 4,000 square feet and was so large and rambling that the day we left I used a downstairs bathroom just to be able to say I had.

It was a classic case of "keeping up with the Joneses." With Susan and I working full-time, we were putting out about $1200 a month in day care fees (we had been recently blessed with the birth of Leah). On top of that, even though we both had high-paying jobs every thing else we earned seemed to be going into that house. A house that we were owned by rather than owning it.

So… once I got my new job and just after the time my second daughter Leah was born, Susan and I moved into the new place with the firm pledge to one another that we would never find ourselves caught in that middle-class trap of living beyond our means.

This new home was kind of a metaphor for that (every pun intended). And so we took on this whole new life with a modified sense of perspective.

Even though I wouldn't admit it, being at a super corporation like Monsanto, there is always the temptation to get "career drunk" on ambition. That carried over a bit into my tenure at ABC, but that was when I started gaining new perspectives in many, many ways.

This new change was a wake-up call in every sense of the word.

RJA: *You mentioned "a couple of things." What was the second?*

Todd: Ah, the more important of the two, because it was about this time (1999) that my second daughter Leah was born. That, to me, was the highlight of our time there. Somehow when you see your daughters born, it gives you sense of completion. And with lovely Leah's arrival, I felt our family was complete. So with the move and with our family officially expanding to four, that was the sense of completion I needed to motivate me yet again.

With two young daughters under the age of five, Susan would now be devoting her days and nights and weekends to being a full-time mom.

RJA: *Did you ever consider having another child after that?*

Todd: Wouldn't have said no, had it taken place, but it didn't. As it is I feel myself to be among the most blessed men on earth. If I have accomplished any one thing in my life of which I am completely and utterly proud, it is having those three phenomenal women in my life.

RJA: *Who will make several appearances later on, I'm happy to say. Back to business, and apparently plenty of it. Suddenly, in the middle of the year 2000, almost two years to the date, you left ABC on very good terms and ended up going as Director of R&D for Metaphore. And here you went again on another career vector; or so it seemed.*

Todd: It was a change, and I have to admit it was by intent. Metaphore was a new pharmaceutical company funded privately through venture capital. They were deep in development of a number of proprietary SOD metal-based drug complexes.

RJA: *SOD. That's Superoxide Dismutase? Right?*

Todd: Right.

RJA: *And catch me if I'm not explaining this correctly. But SOD or* Superoxide dismutase *is an enzyme found in all living cells, but in terms of pain or injury it becomes quickly depleted from the human system.*

Todd: Well, that's technically part of the equation. Specifically, if developed and applied in a bioavailable form, it may be introduced to a human system in pain or debilitation. If it is truly efficacious, it speeds up certain chemical reactions in ways that have been able to accelerate healing—especially for conditions like rebuilding tissue, treating pain and swelling from osteoarthritis, rheumatoid arthritis, sports injuries, gout and even intestinal cystitis.

RJA: *Kind of like a Super Celebrex?*

Todd: Sort of. But more than that, Metaphore was trying to develop SOD mimetic variants to the next level—as a possible treatment for cancer and as a palliative for radiation treatments and other extended uses. I was brought on board as a Director of Drug Development which, when you peeled back the layers on the job description, meant I was responsible for getting these formulae developed in the lab, formed into a clinical product candidate and turned around in time to be ready for rapid assessment as safe to study by the FDA.

That meant I had to spend a ton of time getting these platforms in front of the FDA and running their gamut of approvals. (And it solidified my belief about this agency that fear and opposition accomplish nothing. The earlier you get them involved, and the more you are willing to listen and learn, the better allies they become in the process of approvals.)

RJA: *On the face of it, that's both realistic and a very sound strategy. Did you learn that at Monsanto or ABC? Or was it a gradual process?*

Todd: Well, repetition is the mother of skill and makes you a subject matter expert. Exposure builds relationships. Once you get in the same room and on the same page with people in any regulatory body as important as this, the better your chances of success. It just made sense.

RJA: *Then again, if you're in charge of new product development, and you have a VC group funding you, doesn't that create a different kind of pressure? From my experience venture capital groups are in a high-risk position…followed by a high reward level of expectation. Didn't that create a pretty intense dynamic?*

Todd: Very astute. And yes! That's exactly what it had to be at a very high performance level. Even though we enjoyed optimum flexibility—$2 million to $3 million funding per project—we had to get to the next level quickly. In the venture capital environment you are always facing a burn rate. And we needed to show viability on product potential to get from one pile of money to the next.

The bottom line was a pressure to produce and do so on time. The investors would much rather be on time with a 10% project cost overrun than have a 25% or 30% under budget project and be late. At Metaphore we were virtually joined at the hip to the concept that "time is money." That was the Prime Directive. So I kept that goal in mind and never deviated from that. As a result, I never missed my timelines.

RJA: *It seems, at that point, like you were made for it. I would think you have some superb on-the-job precursors at Monsanto and ABC.*

Todd: No question that at that point, my experience had tempered the steel. Especially having to overcome the power struggle between the lab and the business/marketing camps at ABC, I applied my people skills to always push the agenda forward.

RJA: *So, how did you manage that?*

Todd: At ABC, I just pulled whatever end-runs I found it necessary to do. At Metaphore I was much more in control of the process. Dennis Riley and his team placed a great deal of confidence in me (a position of credibility I believe I had earned). So my actual job description included operational responsibility for half-a-dozen scientists.

The main focus of our work was to refine Metaphore's bio-analytical and drug developmental technology so it could be adapted and utilized at contract research organizations.

RJA: *Would you care to translate that? I mean I think I know what you mean.*

Todd: We were setting up to be what they call an OEM in the field of biochemistry and research technology. In other words The Source. In this case our SOD metal formulations were going beyond their original role as pain killer and palliative and into oncology and what we hoped would be viable treatments for cancer.

So during that three-year process I had to document and author about half dozen *Investigational New Drug* (IND) applications for the FDA. That meant frequent visits to their Oncology, Dermal and Inflammation divisions in DC. And each one had a different set of traps that you had to run. Couple this with the fact that all of our registration work has to be done by external contract research organization (CROs) and all of a sudden you have to find a way to become part of their team. The only way to do this was to be on-site with each and every one of our CRO company partners. So for a while I was spending so much time there I think they started to look upon me as one of the family.

I also had to prepare a number of review documents for Metaphore upper management and then turn around and make oral presentations of our new product concepts and project results to other venture capitalists. That meant I had to be very quick on my feet. You had to be able to credibly answer questions that lead to millions of additional investment dollars. And that, just on its own, was quite a resume builder. I even got listed as "first inventor" on a couple of patent applications.

RJA: *On the surface it sounds like you were on a roll. I mean that's quite a list of accomplishments…and for a drug series with tremendous potential. Sounds almost too good to be true!*

Todd: And what's the old red-flag chestnut? "If something seems too good to be true it usually is." Classic case.

RJA: *Then there was a "fly in the ointment," so to speak?*

Todd: A couple, I'm afraid. And really that's what makes this corner of the science/drug/biochemical universe so tricky to navigate. The stakes are so high. The costs can be prohibitive. And there is always so much pressure to produce. So there are those occasions when the desire to create a winner heads straight onto a collision course with the ethical pathways needed to get there.

RJA: *I'm sensing a collision course between principal and potential. So what went down?*

Todd: A great deal. Since I was responsible for virtually "everything" that came out of Chemistry R&D with respect to its translation into an approvable product by the FDA, I knew what had to come out of our research and what hoops we had to jump through. The FDA was going to require some pretty rigorous, non-biased data sets. So a great deal of testing involving significant numbers would be required, including, in addition to a myriad of other things, toxicology.

At this point, we knew this SOD formulation—whose primary purpose would be as an adjuvant for cancer treatment—had shown some serious potential in a Clinical Phase II trial that was going well.

At the same time the company wanted to position the SOD mimetic franchise in an acute pain product development course. However when I got back the first toxicology reports, I was very concerned. The pre-clinical animal toxicology studies conflicted with many of the data being reported from the pre-clinical animal pharmacology group ... which raised some safety issues that, in my opinion, would have precluded exposure to human subjects.

And since I was the one who had to sign off on the drug package to the FDA, my reputation and credibility were on the line, and there were just some things I couldn't in good conscience ascribe to.

I immediately took my concerns to the Board of Directors at Metaphore and laid them out, but to my utter surprise, they overrode them.

RJA: *That sounds pretty dodgy. Did they do it intentionally? Or was it simply a matter of self-deception?*

Todd: I can't presume to know whether or not they were willing to shelve their scruples and press on. But I do know they were under tremendous financial pressure to bring a winner to market. And people in that position tend to get expedient when it comes to justifying their decisions.

RJA: *Well, you're being very tactful. Would this have been something comparable to what they did in the 1980s to rush the drug AZT to market long before it was proven safe? There are still some allegations that the medicine killed more people than the disease. And I believe there have been several lawsuits over this.*

Todd: That's not a bad comparison. And yes, that was my concern. More than my concern, those were my conclusions based on our findings. I am a data driven scientist. Emotions or financial considerations always need to be removed from the decision tree. I expressed those findings in a presentation I made to the Board of Directors at Metaphore, and apparently they chose not to be "confused by the facts." So it left me no other alternative except to immediately tender my resignation. I also emailed back-up documents to a private account to make sure I had an accurate snapshot of the moment in the event that the future became malleable and fuzzy on the facts.

RJA: *An acid test of integrity that you passed with flying colors.*

Todd: No test for me really: There's right. And there's wrong, and from what I could see this was several kinds of wrong. Anyway, about two years later Metaphore was bought out. Their "star" product failed in multiple clinical trials, and the purchasing entity ended up filing for bankruptcy. So my initial convictions were vindicated.

RJA: *And long before that you had moved on to the next flagship experience in your life—CAMBREX! Is that right?*

Todd: Well, my great relationship with CAMBREX was preceded by what turned out to be a career detour for a few months—back to ABC Laboratories—which, in retrospect, was a kind of comedy of errors that turned out to be a blessing.

RJA: *Are you one of those rare people who can fall into a bucket of swill and come out smelling like a rose? If you are, I'm just a little bit envious.*

Todd: I have to believe there were some "Higher Hands" helping me along through all this. Because after that little crisis of consciousness at Metaphore and my subsequent departure, ABC came back to me with what seemed to be the dream job.

They brought me back to be the President of Pharmaceutical Development along with the suggestion that they were grooming me to run the company (sooner rather than later).

I didn't have to move. I was back on a schedule for which I had already established a pattern. And I was coming back to a company that I had virtually helped raise from the dead. So my personal cachet at that point was pretty stellar, or so I thought.

So it felt, in a way, like I was coming home.

RJA: *Do I hear the deadly silence of the other shoe about to drop?*

Todd: If you did, you're better at this than I was. Anyway, it really came about in the most bizarre set of circumstances. Because about three months into my glorious return to ABC, the powers that be hired a team of efficiency experts to come in on a time-management analysis and breakdown the strengths and weaknesses of the company.

After a couple of weeks and a department-by-department breakdown, they recommended a rather broad set of cutbacks— one of which meant entirely eliminating my department and my newfound executive position along with it. So boom! I got axed for a set of reasons that had nothing to do with me.

Something of a surprise, I can tell you.

RJA: *Had to be devastating. Or was it? You seem to take that kind of stuff pretty much in stride.*

Todd: I've always been reminded of something John F Kennedy once said about the Chinese perception of any tough situation. "In the Chinese (Mandarin) language, there are two characters that form the word *Crisis*. One symbolizes *Danger;* the other, *Opportunity.*"

I think that's a great parable.

And though I know that may not be the precise definition, the truth is it inspired me. So I overcame. And the good stuff happened immediately on the heels of the bad. So things worked out perfectly.

It also didn't hurt in the least that ABC felt so terrible about the decision to let me go that they gave me a terrific severance package, almost as an apology. So I could have done pretty well for quite some time just on the money they paid me to leave.

RJA: *How so? Did you have an ace up your sleeve all this time?*

Todd: Unconsciously if not immediately. One of the best aspects in all my work at ABC and Metaphore came with my ability over the years to network with some pretty impressive people, including a lot of key players at Cambrex. One of them was Cambrex's CEO Gary Mossman.

In size and scope, they were what would be described as a tier two technology corporation—smaller in size and scope than Monsanto but much larger and with a broader sphere of influence by far than ABC. They had about 2000 employees, and somewhere around $600 million in gross annual revenues. So they had leverage, reputation and scope.

RJA: *So, how would you describe Cambrex?*

Todd: In the broadest sense, Cambrex would be described as a "life sciences" company. Its main function is to provide products and services for small molecule Active Pharmaceutical Ingredients (APIs). An API is the molecular "entity" that once compounded in a pill, liquid, or patch and taken according to the prescription, will deliver the cure as reviewed and approved by the FDA. APIs are mostly small molecule synthetic entities, which means chemists and chemical engineers are required for their FDA compliant manufacture.

RJA: *That's pretty tricky stuff. Is this like making things that make things that actually run the world?*

Todd: You could say that. I'm not sure you'd be right. But it sounds close. Anyway, ABC had become what they call a first part collaborator with Cambrex on a couple of projects, and when I came back to head up their Pharmaceutical Development Division, Cambrex invited me to take a seat on their Science Advisory Board.

RJA: *So they already liked you a lot.*

Todd: Well, let me put this way. The day I was let go at ABC, I made a key call to Cambrex, and Gary Mossman brought me on board the very next day.

RJA: *Then you were technically unemployed for about 48 hours.*

Todd: Something like that. Cambrex was branching out into several areas at once, and Gary needed me to come in and help bolster up their pharmaceutical and Early Drug Discovery Division. That meant I had to find ways to take their research and development capabilities and start working with companies during Phase I and Phase II clinical trials.

RJA: *Seems like quite a challenge.*

Todd: And a lot of fun. In fact it was one of the best periods of my life.

RJA: *Do tell. And I mean that. I do want to hear all about it.*

Todd: … Which we should probably do next time.

RJA: *Are we saving the best for last?*

Todd: I don't know. Maybe. But it's all good…all of it.

Note: At this point, I have come to appreciate Todd Johnson's sense of timing. He's not only an excellent storyteller but also someone who relies on his own energy to keep up the pace. If it slows he senses that and calls for us to take a break.

As we close the session, I make a request that we have some photos made for the book. His energy and passion are superb, but I personally believe that they will work best if we pop-in some candid camera shots of the man in his environment.

When I bring it up, Todd gets it right away.

"Like the old interviews you used to find in Playboy and National Geographic."

"Pretty much," I tell him. "I think it will help animate the book."

Instantly he agrees, and we both start to realize that we are collaborating on something that is going to go outside of the box.

At this point, it seems only fitting...

CHAPTER 7

CHANGING LANES PART 2: THE POWER TO CHOOSE

"Todd always saw an opportunity where no one else thought about it, and then just went out and did it. That requires a very special ability to integrate findings and translate them into results."

~ Gary Mossman/Former CEO, CAMBREX

Somewhere in the logical progression of any book, play or screenplay I have to observe that most stories have arcs. In screenwriting, we are told that you need to have three acts in any script and mark them as such. It's almost a forced matrix at times because occasionally you have to assign climaxes where none exist.

In the case of Todd Johnson's saga, it seems to me that we're more like a good old-fashioned serial—cliffhangers in every chapter. Still, it is here that I would probably announce that we are somewhere near the middle of Act II and headed for the most exciting part.

This is not a spoiler alert. It's just what my notes are telling me—those and my interviews with some pretty fascinating people that precede this. I make mention of this because it forms a pattern of achievement. And it follows a covenant that Todd made with himself, "to leave something better than you found it."

That more or less sets the stage for what we are going to discuss next. And that is the continuation of Todd's career arc and what has turned out to be something of a Wellington Cake of a success model.

At this point, it's the most logical comparison I can think of. A Wellington cake is one noted for having unlimited layers. And Todd Johnson and I both note at this point that there is a unique structure to his career in that he had a return engagement in just about every corporate assignment he ever agreed to take on.

RJA: *There seems to have been a pattern in your career in that in the majority of cases (Monsanto being the exception) you were invited back by your former employers with what amounted to an even better deal. So…brought back by popular demand?*

Todd: Yes, it does validate a sense of accomplishment I had that I must have done a pretty good job for these people. And that feels good to me.

RJA: *Case in point: the next company you came to be with, Cambrex. You actually seem to have come over from the paradox at Metaphore on a wave of momentum and high expectations. And their management team headed up by CEO Gary Mossman already had a niche cut out for you.*

Todd: It was definitely a "warm" market due to the contacts I had made at other venues. And yes! Since they had already thought enough of me to put me on their Science Advisory Board, it did have the feeling of coming home. It also didn't hurt that Gary Mossman made me the proverbial "offer I couldn't refuse." So I had quite a bit of momentum for me going-in.

RJA: *Now, Cambrex corporate was (and is) based in New Jersey...*

Todd: They also had offices in North Brunswick, New Jersey, Karlskoga, Sweden, Wiesbaden, Germany, Milan, Italy, Cork, Ireland, Tallinn, Estonia and a few other places. So it was in every possible sense an international operation.

RJA: *And you were able to base out of their offices in Charles City, Iowa—basically back home, so to speak.*

Todd: Close anyway. And I have to admit my Cambrex period was kind of a Golden Era for me. My official title was Director of New Product/New Project Development. But what I really was had more to do with bridging their large scale pharmaceutical manufacturing capability with a more strategic plan to land early Phase I and Phase II clients. Also it was clear that Charles City, was becoming their best in class corporate base of operations. What it meant for me was cutting to the chase of actually finding projects and products that worked for both the client and Cambrex.

Technically I was a "team manager." But my real job was more like that bridge between two worlds—between science/ product technology and the real world of markets and product. It was important to Cambrex that they would be able to state their value to large pharmaceuticals companies. But it was even more imperative that they be able deliver value to micro, small, and mid-cap pharma companies.

What Gary Mossman admitted up front was that he was bringing me in to be his "B.S. Detector" and offer intelligent translation between science, manufacturing, business unit heads and the marketplace. What so often happens in companies like Cambrex was what I had experienced to some degree at ABC— the scientists in the lab don't understand the demands of the marketplace, and so they dig in and start playing the intellectual superiority card with manufacturing and business unit heads.

"There are so many factors you don't understand..." starts to get to be the blocking code the scientists go by. And suddenly things start grinding to a halt replete with tons of in-fighting— not a very popular place to be with the boys in the boardroom, especially when you're trying to build up a pharmaceutical division that is already in one of the most competitive fields in the world.

By then I had a quite a few tools in my bag. So it didn't take long for the science guys to get who I was...and to realize that they couldn't intellectualize their way out of a result. I was there to make everyone, including myself, accountable. It also meant I had to generate a whole series of *white papers,* something for which I had already become pretty well known for doing.

RJA: *Objective analysis feasibility studies.*

Todd: People want to know if you're serious. And White Papers are the best way to show them we've done our homework. Nothing to hide—it's all out there.

RJA: *OK. You're credible. You're on a roll (again). But you've had all that before. So, what made Cambrex so much more of the life and the success model you wanted? Obviously they held you in high regard.*

Todd: For me it was the best of both worlds. I was making great money, and I was able to do most of it without working too hard at it. Not that I ever objected to hard work. But at this point, things were just coming easily to me. You might say I had pretty much gotten into "the zone" where my productivity was concerned.

Gary Mossman and his crew always came to me directly to get a real read on things. I had a lot of credibility with them. Soon I became involved with their Operations Committee. Our division was constantly setting new sales goals and meeting or exceeding them. So everything was clicking. In fact, I had so much flexibility and trust from the company, there were days when I could work at home on my computer—in my pajamas—and accomplish everything I needed to do.

I was my own boss, even though technically I had one.

RJA: *That was Eric Neuffer.*

Todd: Correct. Eric was the Director of Business development for North America Pharmaceutical Division. But unlike my experiences at ABC where the head of the science division felt threatened by me, or Metaphore where they just chose not to listen, Eric had his ego in place and totally got what I could bring to the table. Eric was about eight years younger than I, but from day one, he invited me in to work side-by-side with him, and we became a great team...and great friends.

In fact, one of the things we did best together was to tag team our pitches. Eric is very modest in many ways, but when it counts he's a true extrovert and doesn't know a stranger. He is also very astute in his evaluation of others. So that, combined with my thorough preparation, made us pretty unstoppable when it came to making our case to new prospects...to just about anyone.

RJA: *Eric told me you were great to work with—that you were confident but humble—that you were always mindful of your roots, and that it gave you an exceptional streak of humanity.*

Todd: That's interesting. Because you'd never know Eric was the son of the CEO of a Fortune 500 company—he is so unpretentious, so down-to-earth and one of the most accessible people I have ever met.

RJA: *Eric had many good things to say about you. He said you were intensely focused about knowing everything about every aspect of a business—up and down, front and back. He pointed out the fact that you actually made a point of having such command of a product that you actually knew more about it than the people who had created it.*

Todd: That's just called due diligence in my never-ending quest to be a subject matter expert on everything. For me, that's just a prerequisite for getting on top of things. It's all about mastery of any subject or any task. From my experience, it's not just the best way, it's the only way.

RJA: *He also emphasized your skills as one of the few people who exceeds expectations at everything he does. I believe he said: "Todd particularly excels at being able to take a complex process – and distill it down into such a simple format that the average customer would understand." Add to that the fact that he said you came up with the right answer and the right path for everything they tagged you with.*

Todd: We had a pretty complex set of strategies as I recall. But what made it really work was having people like Eric and Gary (and the site Director at Cambrex Charles City – Joe Nettleton) there with you all the way. We did some really great things the first time I was there. And yeah, of course, if you have to "dumb it down" a bit to get it understood, then you absolutely do so! I like to think we explained things that fourth graders could understand without coming across as insulting or condescending.

The marketing, fulfillment, and project management graveyards are filled with products that couldn't get their message across. That applies in particular to those in the contract development of ethical drugs and pharmaceutical formulations. So I spent my fair share of time making sure we got our message across by any means necessary.

RJA: *That would make it seem as if you were working non-stop. But you had some pretty good times too, or so I understand. You were key member of a crack team of eight business development people, travelling all over the world on behalf of Cambrex, delivering dissertations in front of large groups of smart people, and even playing in few "celebrity" golf tournaments along the way.*

Todd: Thank my dear old dad for helping make me "fearless." Crowds have never bothered me. And I truly enjoy being the business development group's spokesman who's able to articulate what we've been working on with operations to develop. After all, why create a great concept or a winning development strategy and then not be able to put it over? I knew I/we could. So I was always "that guy." Besides, I'm sure some people might have showed up just to see if I could walk my talk.

As far as the trips and golf were concerned, for the most part I truly relished the experiences I had. For a few years I got to travel to some of the glamor spots in the world—Sweden, Italy, Ireland, Eastern Europe.

And I loved playing in the tournaments, probably because at a level of actually participating, golf is my favorite sport in the world. And Gary and Eric always wanted me on their tournament teams. So I played a great deal.

RJA: *About your golf game, ahem… Eric Neuffer told me about the first time you played in a tournament. At the time you hadn't picked up a stick in about three years. And you went out and shot an 82 or something…and you were really upset because you didn't do better?! I mean nobody lays off golf for three years and then shoots an 82. But you did. And then it bothered you that you didn't shoot a lower score. I mean, what's up with that?!*

Todd: Well, I guess I have high standards or I'm a bit competitive. Critical assessment is always a good thing.

RJA: *You think?! I mean, I know you're a scratch golfer and all that…*

Todd: Have been. I am definitely not scratch at this point – just ask my Country Club league teammates. I could be again if I would just spend enough time at it. I love golf. And I've always had a natural affinity for the game.

RJA: *So how did you get into it?*

Todd: I came late to the game really. When I was in the 8th grade (13 years-old) I saved my money and paid $15 for a set of golf clubs. Back in the 1970s the local country club allowed juniors to play for $40 a year flat fee. So every summer I used to play 36 holes a day, almost every day, or as often as I could.

RJA: *Another point of obsession? I guess I should say "passion." You're passionate about it.*

Todd: Repetition is the mother of skill, especially in that sport. I was on my high school varsity golf team for four years. And it's always been my favorite sport to play, because it's the most honest test of your ability to excel under pressure.

RJA: *How so? I know it's a rhetorical question. I just want to hear your philosophy on it.*

Todd: Well, for me golf is more than a sport. It's a special journey into self-discovery—because it's just you, the ball and the course. No place to hide. No one to blame or praise but yourself. For me it's the truest test of character someone can have. And then there's the course itself. So many times you're surrounded by this incredible imprint of Nature, and history…and tradition. I mean I've played at places like the National next door to Shinnecock Hills,

Redstone Golf Club, Torrey Pines—places where they've played the U.S. Open or standing PGA tour stops.

My ultimate bucket list would be to play the Old Course at St. Andrews in Scotland. You're walking on the same ground as the greats—Nicklaus, Palmer, Gary Player, Bobby Jones and Harry Vardon. And you can almost feel the presence of the entire birthplace of what many call "The Greatest Game."

RJA: *I didn't mean to digress. It just seemed to fit the whole profile of what your life was like then.*

Todd: It's not a digression really. It was all a part of the high-profile lifestyle I was living at the time. I was one of Cambrex's top performers. And Gary Mossman always brought me in to play in his executive tournaments. They were also the ideal places to network with important people in with accounts we were trying to land or key customers we were trying to reward with a big "thank you."

This was also a period where we hit all kinds of milestones at Cambrex. We exceeded every sales target I was involved in. I was in that unique position of being able to advise C-Suite Wall-Street level functions from the comfort of my own living room. I was reporting directly to a great supervisor, had access to the Cambrex Board of Directors, hit my performance goals early and often, and had no fear of retribution when I spoke my mind. So this was truly the best of all possible worlds.

RJA: *Sounds like the perfect place to be? And you were definitely on a roll for three years at least—from 2004 to 2007. So what changed?*

Todd: Good question. And I had to think about that for a while. I can only answer that by saying it was that first inkling I began to have that I would never be quite at peace with myself working for another company or in an environment over which I did not have significant measure of control. I started to have that longing to be captain of my own ship. It may not have manifested in its entirety. But it came up full force when I got an offer to become CEO of a new start-up pharmaceutical company called-KemPharm, Inc.

RJA: *I believe KemPharm is still around today.*

Todd: Yes it is. They've managed to stay the course despite a few bumps along the way. And in a way, it has a new incarnation.

RJA: *But it was something different when you helped it to come into being. So how did that take place?*

Todd: On the way to helping Cambrex become a major player in the contract manufacturing pharmaceutical field, I made several connections with other companies—one of which was New River Pharmaceuticals, and a man named Dr. Travis Mickle. Travis in many ways seemed like the perfect fit for me. He was setting up KemPharm, Inc. in Coralville, Iowa. He was a PhD and a University of Iowa alumnus. So, in so many ways we spoke the same language.

On top of that, Travis and KemPharm had a couple of intriguing new molecules in hand, and an overall platform that that suggested to me that they could not miss in the high stakes arena of drug development. Add to that the fact that Travis invited me to come in at the top. And since I've always been a risk taker, I decided to take the plunge.

RJA: *What did it for you? Did he make you an offer you couldn't refuse? What was the allure of this company after all?*

Todd: I think the allure for someone like me was the ability to build something. I've always had a pioneering nature. I like to break new ground. And I was seeing the brass ring in front of me to truly see if I was as good as I thought.

As it turned out, Travis made me an offer I should have refused. But he did make it sound, on the face of it, that he was bringing me in basically to replace him as the head of the company and run KemPharm. I was brought in to be the company's CEO and even convinced to become a significant shareholder that would seem to give me added leverage. Susan and I contributed just shy of 10% of the original start-up capital.

RJA: *On the surface this seems extraordinarily risky. Did you run it by Susan and the family?*

Todd: Yes, of course I did. I even took a trip for a week to think things over. And I have to admit it took some convincing. I mean Susan has always had my back. So she ultimately went along with it, although I know she had some major concerns, as did the rest of her family. Nevertheless, they backed my play, and I went ahead with it.

As I mentioned just a moment ago, KemPharm was starting out with some promising product technology—one that from where I was sitting offered tremendous market potential.

So I came on board with the responsibility of raising venture capital for a new company and for helping to refine, research and develop these new product technologies and get them ready for Phase I clinical trials.

I felt it was understood that I was supposed to be given complete autonomy, with the idea that Travis could focus on immense R&D challenges required to get a new chemical entity into its first Human Clinical trial. But shortly after I arrived I came to realize that my new position was the reverse of what I'd had at every other company.

RJA: *In what way?*

Todd: Well, where I had no real title but tremendous leverage and responsibility at ABC, Cambrex and even Monsanto, all I had at KemPharm was a title with virtually no power whatsoever. I was expected to secure funding for this "hot new company," but was not allowed to operate without running everything by Travis. Soon enough, this became my first real insight into working with a brilliant owner/founder who legally controlled every aspect of the company.

(I did my job, by the way, and managed to raise between $2 million and $5 million in new funding in a fairly brief period. But even then I was starting to see the warning signs.)

RJA: *Warning signs? Bait and switch?*

Todd: Maybe not by conscious intent, but it was there. Because it didn't take me long to realize that Travis had no intention whatsoever of stepping aside with respect to the non-R&D side of the company. He was going to be around and approve or unilaterally veto every move I wanted to make. He fully intended to be very hands-on in his management style. And as long as he was, I was going to be nothing more than a figurehead. It was a terrible place for a person like me because it was literally viewed as a requirement for me to be there when we took meetings and made pitches to potential investors. In fact, many times we were questioned what my true role and responsibility at KemPharm was.

To complicate matters further, the one formulation they had that seemed to be effective against ADHD, appeared to have striking molecular similarities to the active ingredients in Vyvanse. So at best we might have been looking at a "me too" product; or at worst, a patent infringement. Either way it was not something that traditional venture capitalists were willing to take a chance on.

So it became apparent to me that things may not end well for KemPharm. The risk curve had steepened. Coupled with the fact that I was figuratively depressed and hated going into the office everyday, I still had to reconcile with Susan that we had made a very substantial investment in something that wasn't going very well for me. This is not to say that KemPharm didn't have a future, but rather it became clear that Todd Johnson did not have a future with KemPharm.

RJA: *Sounds like you had already begun laying down your exit path in a lot of ways. And I suppose that meant cutting your losses.*

Todd: Yes! And yes! For me, it was a lot like someone had just lobbed a live grenade into our family dinner. So I literally had to face a King Solomon's dilemma of sticking around and trying to make the most of a bad deal, or run the risk of losing my day-today operational assets to our initial investment and all my stock options, or just biting the bullet and moving on.

So after I made my decision I went straight to Travis Mickle and told him. "I'm just not the right guy for the job…At this point I'm just an expensive burn rate, and neither one of us is getting our money's worth."

RJA: *Pretty up front, I have to say. How did he take it?*

Todd: Not surprisingly, he didn't fight it. We had become toxic for each other and we both knew that if the company was to survive I needed to leave. I felt dirty, I felt ashamed, and I felt like I had screwed up in a major league way. It was about as low as I had ever been in my life.

Once again, I'm happy to say, I didn't burn my bridges. I agreed not to cause problems with the group of investors that I represented. In exchange, Travis kept me on the Board of Directors. And we both agreed that we would keep an open line of communication between us. This was really a no-brainer for me to stay on good terms with them. I would always keep Kem-Pharm's best interest at heart. So, essentially, I maintained the connection and the show of faith. So I made no bonfires and managed to keep a friend in the process.

RJA: *Another bridge "not burned." I have to admit, I'm astounded at how you managed to do it. It's an art form.*

Todd: So almost a year to the date, I said good-bye to Kem-Pharm, called up Steve Klosk, the new CEO at Cambrex (and good friend from my first time at Cambrex)—and he put something in front of me that was even more lucrative and promising than before. And even though I had taken a bit of a hit with my career sidestep to KemPharm, I knew that I could and would recover in a major way by coming back to Cambrex.

RJA: *By that time, though, I understand that your old boss Gary Mossman had already moved on.*

Todd: Yes, he had. Still, I had so many other good relationships that remained intact. By the way, Gary also made a substantial investment in KemPharm when I became CEO. He in fact put together a consortium that tried to buy a majority interest in KemPharm but we couldn't come to terms. I often wonder if Pomifera® would have ever come about if I would have been supported as CEO by Gary's investor group.

By that time, Cambrex were now so aware of what I could do that I came back in for even more money and was brought on board specifically to be their Global Director of Controlled Substances. It was something of a pressure cooker, but I was ready for it.

RJA: *I know the reference pretty well—and that it's a very "hot" place to be in the world of Big Pharma. I also know it's a terrifyingly Brave New World out there. But you might want to explain exactly what that means to those are not yet up on all things scientific.*

Todd: There is a fairly simple description of a complex issue. And it's this: Controlled substances are prescription formula drugs that may be highly effective in treating a given disease or pathology. But…they may have issues of patient addiction that require restricted usage over a prolonged period of time. Control is the key word. The intent is to control the drugs such that they are taken as prescribed and not stolen or diverted and sold on the black market.

The best example of those would be something like painkillers (like Vicodin) or opioid-based products like Morphine, Fentanyl, Oxycontin, or Vicodin. They're highly effective for certain things, especially pain relief and chronic or terminal illness. But they can also be very addictive.

So several government agencies as well as the World Health Organization (WHO) all tend to get involved in supply chain management from the poppy fields to the regulation of dosages and frequency of use. And that can become something of a minefield.

RJA: *So, this was what you were brought back to Cambrex to oversee and develop?*

Todd: Yes—a wholehearted commitment to really expand and grow. It's a multi-billion dollar business. But it's something that requires both conscience and restraint to develop and oversee the right kind of product. So I like to believe they brought me in because I could bring the right approach to research, business development, and product fulfillment.

RJA: *And I understand you were brought back, as they say, by popular demand?*

Todd: Well, controlled substances can be a minefield to navigate with the FDA. And since I knew the workings of that agency as well as anyone could within Cambrex, I think they believed I was the right person to handle it. I was also brought on board as Director of R&D to get it back to a practical functioning body.

As so often happens there came to be a lot of barriers—if not actual walls—between R&D, manufacturing, and business.. It had become very dysfunctional. So I had to apply some of "Todd's Rules of the Road" to get them back into a working relationship.

I had to convince the boys in the lab that business was not the enemy—that this was not a zero-sum game. Fortunately, my reputation had preceded me. I had my PhD in Chemistry to make me credible with the science guys, and eventually we tore down the wall.

RJA: *Then you were wearing several hats at the same time.*

Todd: I was. And it was totally by design. When I came back we had a gentlemen's agreement that I would use any means necessary to get R&D back fully functioning again, and then in a year or two train my replacement. So my limited tenure was entirely by design.

I know that sounds a bit bizarre. But it's not. As we've discussed earlier in our conversations, the one way to make sure you never go anywhere is by making yourself irreplaceable. And that in business can be the kiss of death.

RJA: *You certainly had no problem with that. Apparently you like cloning yourself…or at least grooming others to jump in. So once you accomplished "mission impossible" one more time, did you again feel the need to move on?*

Todd: Well no, it was something completely different. And in a way, I even surprised myself with what came next.

RJA: *In what way? So what did come next?*

Todd: I think, perhaps for the first time in my life, I might have let my ego get the best of me. I mean, here I was more or less Cambrex's Ambassador without portfolio and "The Man Behind the Curtain" for two of its divisions. And yet, I still felt as if I needed to move up to the next level.

RJA: *I don't think that would have happened out of the blue. Did something trigger your decision?*

Todd: Yes, as a matter of fact, something did. And what prompted it was something I discovered along the way. Somewhere around the beginning of 2010, I was acting as the face of the franchise in so many ways, making quarterly reports to the BOD of Cambrex, I was a full member of the Operations Committee, was looked to as the technical expert for mergers and acquisitions, traveling all over the world and conducting containment design seminars with groups such as *The International Society of Professional Engineers.* So I thought I was at the top of my game when "wham" I find out my counterpart in Cambrex's Milan [Italy] office was performing essentially the same function and making more than twice my salary.

Well…perceptions of worth are relative indeed. But I knew this much: I was delivering the goods. And nobody could do it better. So, I took the leap and went into to Steve Klosk and the Executive Committee and put in my bid to become COO of Cambrex.

Perhaps it was hubris, but I figured it was time to stand up for what I felt I could do best.

RJA: *I'm not quite sure I understand why you think it would be hubris. It seems to me that you've been the "smartest man in the room" in almost every company you've been involved with. (And that's not just me talking. It's the people I've interviewed.) So why not stand up for yourself? Especially since you just left a CEO post from another company (KemPharm) to go back to Cambrex. Surely they had to know that and take that into consideration.*

Todd: Well you may have seen it that way. And maybe Travis Mickle saw it that way. And (who knows) had Gary Mossman still been there, it might have been a different story.

As it was, the people at the top at Cambrex at that time didn't see me that way. To them I speculate that I was that secret weapon—that Michael Clayton in their group who could work miracles but who was just a little too "different" to take a major management position in the company.

I know they would have been quite happy to have me stay on and were disappointed that I was leaving. But at that point, I felt as if I had completed my contract. Remember I was originally brought in to accomplish certain milestones. And by the middle of 2010 I had done that. So…by that time I was being approached again by KemPharm to come back, this time on a more realistic basis.

RJA: *I've got to tell you, I think I may rename you, Todd the Cat, because you've certainly got nine-lives where your career is concerned. Anyway this perfectly fits your career pattern: going back in where you were before, even more in demand and at a higher fee structure.*

Todd: Well, remember I was still very heavily invested in Kem-Pharm in every sense of the word. And this time, Travis and I got on the same page about what my role was to be. So here I was yet again brought in as a problem solver. I was going to be their COO. So I was very much aware that I was part of the decision chain and not the final word. KemPharm was also better funded, and they had real operational deliverables that were not being met.

In the purest sense of the word, my title should have been CGID (Chief Get It Done) because that was the closest to my new job description. Technically, however, I was definitely brought in to get KemPharm's new entry into the very lucrative field of controlled substance pharmaceuticals—specifically a non-addictive, highly effective painkiller back on a clinical development timeline that matched up with current burn rate. If I missed the timeline, KemPharm could have easily run out of cash prior to getting this exciting molecule into the clinic.

The product currently under formulation, development and test was called KP-201. And it had the very special potential of being a non-abusive, non-addictive form of hydrocodone (something that could compete successfully with leading painkillers like Norco, Vicodin or Lorcet, but without the innately addictive nature that stigmatizes so many opioid-based products).

Since KemPharm was already locked in a technology hassle with Shire Pharmaceuticals over our flagship (ADHD) product, they needed a market winner. And this KP-201 formulation promised to be just that.

The tricky part is that the horizons for these products making it from the lab to the marketplace can often take the better part of a decade. That partly explains their high cost at the consumer/patient level. Some companies have occasionally ransomed their future just to get one groundbreaking product to market. So it definitely comes at a cost.

RJA: *Was that the allure in all this? I think that all this would be heady wine indeed, knowing that what you're doing might have the ability to change people's lives for the better.*

Todd: I think that's what gets you up in the morning—that ability to make a difference. And that was the appeal of KemPharm for me, knowing that I would be at the top of the decision chain and not somewhere in the middle trying to give life to someone else's initiatives.

RJA: *But I'm assuming that's not exactly what happened. Otherwise you'd still be there.*

Todd: And you would be right. I suppose I should have enjoyed a sense of completion. I was invested. I was an officer of the company. I now had a realistic working relationship with the head of the company. I was COO. And I knew my role—to be KemPharm's liaison to manufacturing and all things related to drug development, and participated with Wall Street as required. I was absolutely at the top of my game when it came to translating science to the rigors of FDA regulated drug development and manufacturing and making that articulate presentation of ideas and translate it into Moneyball.

Still I am the first to admit that when I got there, I felt somehow as if there was a huge piece missing out of my life—at least my professional life.

Don't get me wrong. It was everything I was looking for—on paper. And I was more than doing my job. I was doing the work of three people. I was at the office or working at home 60 hours a week, week-in-week-out. I even made a few trips to Wall Street to network with the serious funding that we were going to have to raise to keep the company moving ahead.

To be perfectly candid, I didn't like the vibe on Wall Street at all. It was slick. It was superficial. And there was constant agitation to feed the greed without any consideration of for keeping your soul. And that's when I started to realize that this wasn't a world I wanted to spend the rest of my life in.

What really struck me like a thunderbolt was the fact that, despite my seeming success on paper, I was feeling mentally and emotionally damaged. And I wasn't enjoying life anymore.

RJA: *Wow! That's got to be tough. I mean, you get to the top of your game and find you've hit your head on the ceiling. Suddenly you're starting to lead what Henry David Thoreau described as, "A life of quiet desperation." So what was missing?*

Todd: For lack of a better definition it had to be the fact that I missed being able to tap into my God-given ability to create something of value; to tinker with the unknown. I was bored to tears. Lots of square pegs into square holes. Also, in the fall of 2010 Uncle Don's wife, Aunt Dorothy, died and inevitably the idea of hedgeballs kept occupying my mind during the drudgery of my day-to-day.

The scary thing is that for anyone else, it might have been a temptation to capitulate—just take the money, head to the golf course and go live the life of a country club cadaver. But that was absolutely not where I wanted this rainbow to end. So I knew I would have to make a change…and soon.

RJA: *Obviously you did. So, how quickly did you mange to make your move?*

Todd: It's funny. And this has always been the case in my life. About the time I decided to make a move, I reconnected with my longtime friend Erik Tjaden. He had recently established his new company Tjaden Biosciences, LLC And they had racked up several "wins" since he had founded his company.

Erik had developed some niche product technologies that were hugely successful. And so when I reconnected with him in 2012, he told me it was just the right time.

I believe he said something to the effect that he had stretched his product technologies all the way out and wanted to diversify.

"My business is flat-lining," I believe he said, or words to that effect. And he emphasized the fact that he had maxed out his revenue stream—at least with his current product technologies.

It wasn't necessarily that. But I knew what he meant, because there is a saturation point in any company where you either have to diversify your technologies or you start to stagnate. And in the worlds of technology, pharmacology and chemistry, things can get pretty Darwinian.

I was already on the Board of Tjaden Biosciences. So when Erik invited me to come over to help him research and develop some daring new science technologies, I started to recognize this as a sign.

And that's when I had my Eureka moment! I had been sitting on a treasure trove all this time.

I thought to myself (and later to Erik) if you really want to go where no one has gone before and explore a daring new technology, I have just the one for you—one that may open up a whole new universe of possibilities.

And its name is Pomifera®!

> *"I have a great story that reveals Todd's true character in so many ways. One time when I was visiting him in Columbia, Missouri, we were running late to catch a flight out of Kansas City, and so Todd said: "I have a way to get us there quickly, but we have to put the pedal to the metal. No worries, it is like the wild west out here." So we jumped in our cars and acted like the Interstate was the Autobahn all the way to KC International Airport. I was following him in my rented car, going well over 90 MPH all the way, when we both got zapped from a State Police airplane above and pulled over by a Missouri State Trooper. Todd not only called ahead to make sure I could still get on my flight, he also made one of the most articulate arguments I've ever seen to get me (not him) out of the ticket. He took full responsibility for it, trying to convince the trooper that he had led me astray. It was an epic apology. Unfortunately, it didn't work, but Todd gave it everything he had. He was only concerned about my wellbeing and not his own. That, for me, speaks volumes."*
>
> *~ Eric Neuffer*

CHAPTER 8

A LEAP OF FAITH

"Todd Johnson is very smart and very quick on the draw. He is fearless, and he uses that fearlessness to make converts. When I brought him on board with me at Tjaden, I wanted him to help make us more entrepreneurial. Who knew it would lead to hedge apples and Pomifera? Well, maybe Todd did. Maybe he knew it all along..."

~ Erik Tjaden/CEO, Tjaden Biosciences

After this much time, I notice certain qualities about Todd Johnson. Principal among them is the innate sense of loyalty and friendship he extends to the people he values in his life. They are not large in number. But they all have in common such qualities as depth of character, intelligence and integrity. And they have earned his trust.

Erik Tjaden is such a man.

The mural I have been able to assemble from several sources is one of an unbreakable bond—a brotherhood if you will—that will withstand anything. By now, one is aware of the journey they have shared and the life they have in common—the Midwest (Iowa) roots, the University of Iowa undergraduate education and the PhDs in Chemistry from Indiana University—and, on occasion, the same company banner, even though their respective roles were different. Different as well, has to be the personal style each man brings to the table, one that seems to be appreciated (if not celebrated) by both.

As Todd is both effusive and something of a scientific gunslinger, Erik Tjaden is both circumspect and measured in the majority of his decisions. And yet, when that moment of truth presents itself, each man enjoys the complete confidence of the other. It is corroboration at least of the theory that in some very important ways, opposites do attract.

These men have had a level of trust and respect that has weathered decades and dozens of points of contact. That brings us to that place in their journey in 2012 where Erik and Todd both realized that their time to work together had arrived.

This point of critical mass is where the story of Pomifera® truly comes to life—the virtual sprouting of a concept planted decades, if not centuries, earlier.

RJA: *OK, Todd. So, let's backtrack to 2012. You have just come to a phase at KemPharm where you are their COO. They have a viable drug pending called KP-201 that offers many of the same benefits of a hydrocodone-based substance like Vicodin (but without the addictive nature). And they had achieved some level of stability, so that they would probably survive. But you didn't feel you could if you continued as what you felt was becoming a straw man for the company. So… you decided to save your sanity (if not your soul) and leave. How did they take it? After all, you were their COO?*

Todd: Well, they wanted me to stay. No question. And God only knows I was (and still am) heavily invested. So just in terms of economic leverage there was a great deal of pressure for me to stay the course there. But as I said, I was dying inside. So I knew I had to move. That's why Erik's offer to join him came at the perfect time.

Once again, I'm still a significant shareholder of KemPharm common stock, the company went public in 2015 (NASDAQ symbol: KMPH) and their drug candidate KP-201 was recently approved by the FDA as Apadaz™. So, even now we have a connection, and I'm rooting for them for all the right reasons. I like to think they are working for me instead of the other way round.

Still, by the time 2012 came around I had come to realize that I was done with corporate America and pretty much all it stood for as far as my tolerance levels were concerned.

By that time, I had come to recognize my true entrepreneurial spirit, and staying on someone else's payroll and dancing to the tunes they played was a lockdown for my future. My only hope would have been to become the biggest jack in the box. But it would still be "The Box," and I would still be inside it. And clearly my future was as far away from big corporate captivity as I could get, and with it came all the freedom of movement that implies.

That's when I came to realize that Tjaden was the right move for me. And I think both Erik and I knew it.

The better news was that I was joining a longtime friend and colleague with whom I shared all the same values. Tjaden Biosciences was literally in my own backyard—Burlington is 30 minutes from my house. And I knew I would have all the freedom of movement and decision-making that I needed. So, in every sense of the word, I was coming home.

RJA: *However, in monetary ways, I believe it came at a price I think you took a bit of a pay cut to do it.*

Todd: …In more ways than one, I can assure you. I also learned a long time ago that no amount of money can ease the pain if you know you're in the wrong place. So that was a risk I was willing to take. And Erik was ready to roll the dice with me. He needed some fresh "perspectives," on new ways to grow the business at Tjaden Biosciences. But I don't think he was entirely expecting what I brought to the table next.

RJA: *Pomifera®.*

Todd: Yeah. Talk about your long shot. I have to say that in my heart of hearts I didn't think it was. I had been researching Pomifera off and on for all these years. I had done a lot of homework up to that point. So I had that one in my hip pocket.

But in all fairness to Erik and to his original reasons for our getting together in the first place, I didn't jump in with it until after at least six to eight months after coming aboard.

First, I had to honor the fact that I was there to evaluate Tjaden Biosciences' current market position, and develop new product marketing strategies based on available technologies.

At the time, Tjaden had developed a niche, but attractive, market in radiochemical synthesis and customized radiochemical technology—specifically Carbon 14 radiotracers. These are the ones that determine fractures in all kinds of things. It's a trouble-shoot failsafe testing system but very necessary – still the Gold

Standard with respect to metabolism studies required by the FDA and EPA. We were also trying to expand in tritium-radiolabelled products and University Research compounds. Even today, Erik calls it a boring technology. But as you noted earlier, these are all the tiny gears that truly drive the world.

So, when I came aboard my primary task was to use that base in synthetic chemistry to develop new markets related to Tjaden's core competencies. That meant a great deal of exploration. It also meant that I was able to bring all my experiences at places like Metaphore, ABC and KemPharm to the table. So I was very aware of what product corridors we might want to consider and which ones we should probably avoid.

Pharmaceutical and drug technologies offer tremendous potential. But the field as you know by now tends to be over-sold...and crowded with some major players. The potential for patent overlap can get very tricky. And you generally need some deep pocket funding to prepare, test and run your traps with the FDA. At our level that would have meant some investment, banker interest, or at the very least venture capital.

In the beginning, I have to admit, all options were still on the table. However, having run through all of the hoops with respect to raising venture capital I truly was hesitant to try to take Tjaden Biosciences down that path.

But given the fact that just five years later it was already in pretty good shape as far as its capital payback was concerned, trying to raise additional venture capital would have certainly come with its own set of demands, many of which would be time sensitive. So I think we both agreed that we would want a technology that would leave us in control of our own destiny.

I think Erik felt, as did I, that we wanted to develop some-thing inside that we could also subsidize with our own discre-tionary funds.

RJA: *That had to narrow your avenues of potential. Or did it?*

Todd: Well, I think anytime you decide to be in control of your own destiny, you are better off for the decision. At the same time, it did force us to be resourceful. It meant being diligent in our research and burning some midnight oils. And there were some times in those first six months that we spent quite a few 60-hour plus workweeks.

It's not altogether unusual when you're involved in chemical research and product testing. And I was working beside an abso-lute equal where our command of chemistry was concerned. So the communication was stellar. We had been tested in the fires of trial and error. And I was able to bring every tool I had into this new challenge.

RJA: *Seems to me that picking a winner would have been* a fait accompli. *But from what I can tell, you didn't much like the options you were coming up with. Otherwise you probably would have taken another direction.*

Todd: …Not that we hadn't been trying. And we were looking at a couple of other possibilities. But to that point, nothing quite fit the model.

I think maybe the "aha moment" came when I started to realize that everything we were working on had either some pos-sible patent overlap or issues of relative toxicity that were eventu-ally going to prove problematic or that would render us unable to grow the existing business. Those had always been the "normal" challenges we had faced at other companies with deeper pockets. And they were cropping up with us at Tjaden as well. Not that it was all that unusual; in most instances these are just some of the many perils of product development...especially in technology.

Still, at some point the light went on. And it occurred to me that we would be better off working on a product straight from Mother Nature—one that, if positioned properly, would not be subject to same intense scrutiny required by the FDA for drug development.

RJA: *GRAS is* "Generally Regarded As Safe." *So that's when a product virtually qualifies as a food or basic natural element. Was this an instinct, or simply a matter of the process of elimination?*

Todd: Natural products are a good place to look for GRAS. However, "natural" is replete with all kinds of toxic plants and aanimals. And let's face it, instincts are only as good as the science that supports them. So you still have to go through a careful, measured, and thoughtful scientific process.

Then again, I'll be the first to admit that the guardian angel of Uncle Don Prevo had been out there somewhere on a cloud in my subconscious (probably dancing up and down juggling a hedgeball or two).

So I came up with a proposal on Pomifera®. And on a flight to an Isotopes Convention in Frankfurt, Germany in 2012, I hit Erik with what I have come to call "Dreams at 35,000 Feet," which was my first full court press on Pomifera®.

RJA: *Did it come as a surprise? Or was he expecting it? What was his reaction?*

Todd: Erik has known me long enough to realize my capacity for the outrageous. He also knows that I am pretty scrupulous when it comes to doing my homework. So, I think his first reaction was something like, "Hedge apples, huh? Well, let's see what we come up with."

RJA: *Somehow I suspect that might probably the shorthand version.*

Todd: Well…it was a long trip to Europe. So, we had time to discuss everything. I would have expected nothing less. Rightly so, Erik pushed back hard on several points which required me to provide go – no go gates for him as the financier of a crazy project like Pomifera®. Erik also came to realize pretty quickly that I was serious about my proposal. So all options were certainly on the table.

The first one was the fact that I was going to have to create a product model based in real science…and that we were going to have to establish a product model before we set up a business model. That meant I was going to have to spend some time, effort and at least a respectable amount of research capital to get to the heart of the true nature of Pomifera®. I knew it was there. I was also equally certain that the true "magic bullet" inside its chemistry hadn't been discovered yet.

So that's where we agreed to start the next part of the journey.

RJA: *That was part of your decision on the plane trip…*

Todd: And after we got to the convention in Frankfurt. Perhaps not surprisingly, after Erik and I had agreed to get started on this, we had a pretty momentous collision course with history while we were there.

While we were at the hotel in Germany, a little disaster in Libya took place when Islamic extremists overran the American Embassy in Benghazi and murdered four of the American Staff including our Ambassador J. Christopher Stevens.

RJA: *On September 11, 2012. The irony was not lost on me as it was on some—a dreadful day in every sense of the word—and a direct offshoot of the "Arab Spring."*

Todd: It certainly had its ripple effect in Europe, as those events so often do. And fortunately I was able to anticipate what to do.

The reason I did is because I had been in Europe when international calamities had taken place in the past and remembered being stranded for days on end, in Limbo and unable to leave.

Fortunately, I was up early and caught the news right as it happened. So I woke Erik up and said something to the effect that: "I don't know what you're going to do but I'm on the next plane out of here in four hours. Otherwise, we could be stuck here for days."

One quality of true friendship that renders it unique is the ability to be forthright with one another at all times. Erik got it immediately. We both jumped on the next United flight. And as it turned out, we made it back just before the shockwaves from the disaster hit the travel tables everywhere. (Fortunately, we had lifted off by then.) We actually got the last seats on the first flight and the next flight back to the states was cancelled.

RJA: *So…bullet dodged. And I assume you took that to be a good omen, since timing is very much the parent of opportunity meeting intention.*

Todd: It was certainly an indication that we were on the same page. And our decision to forge ahead was one framed with such an historical milestone that I wasn't ever about to forget it.

So we took all appropriate initiatives the moment we got back. We incorporated, and I immediately set up a research model for our proposed technology.

RJA: *From what you told me earlier, I more or less know what each of you brought into this new relationship and new company. You brought your scientific expertise, your research, market savvy, and your absolute belief in what amounted to one of Mother Nature's castoffs? And Erik brought the financial and corporate underpinnings. That was quite a leap of faith on both your parts, but particularly on his—it seems to me.*

Todd: I think that's a pretty accurate appraisal. Erik did bring all of the funding. He underwrote the cost of all this. We also set up Osage Healthcare, Inc. (the corporation that holds the Pomifera® trademark) with the understanding that I would put in all the sweat equity and also be the largest individual stockholder—no matter what. Erik and Tjaden Biosciences would remain silent partners in all this.

We established "reasonable" timetables for product development, testing, findings, product profiling, projected project launches and capital payback horizons. We also dedicated ourselves to setting up an intelligent research model.

RJA: *That must have meant getting you back into the lab in a very big way.*

Todd: Yep! I was heading off to do my "mad scientist" thing… and devoting what would amount to my full time going after it. I was going to have to dig hard, dig deep, and bring all of my PhD in Chemistry chops with me to pull it off.

That would require some detective work coupled with Folklore playing all the while in the back of my mind. And once we uncovered the secret, we could then shift gears and decide if, when and how we might make a viable product line out of it.

The timing and energy were all right with me. As long as my overhead and living expenses were being met, I was willing to do whatever it took to unlock the true secret of Pomifera®.

In fact my flirtations with Pomifera® had ebbed and flowed for many years. I picked up spots of information on it—the Israeli study in 1995, reciting its nutritional content and potential benefits; its rumored uses in veterinary medicine for skin conditions on small animals (dogs and cats); there were the usual anecdotal folk remedies and even rumors of using the pulp from hedge apples as a kind of experimental large breed dog food (one that might have been nutritious but offered very little appeal to the dogs themselves).

There were increasing amounts of data I found in peer revue journals that showed data on compounds extracted from hedge apples. And there were even some failed attempts by small cottage-industry level businesses to make a go of it. There were mounting volumes of information on "Maclura Pomifera" but nothing definitive enough to make a viable product for broad level consumption at any level that could be determined consistent. Supply chain was a huge issue. Erik kept wondering how in the hell was I going to get enough hedge apples to sustain a real business?

From everything I could determine these were evaluations made from the pulp. And whatever came out of them was far from the finished product.

I was always of the belief that we needed to take a deeper dive on this. But before I could do that, I would have to go through the disciplines necessary to determine what wouldn't work on the way to finding what would. That meant kissing a lot of frogs along the way.

The hardest part of any research is knowing that the frogs you're kissing all wear familiar faces. And yet you have to suspend your disbelief and go through that process of elimination. So…even though I was pretty convinced that the fleshy part of the pulp was not the answer, I still went through the laborious process of crystallizing, characterizing and itemizing every component in it.

The way I did that was to go back and applied the traditional scientific method: taking three major components in the hedge apples and breaking them down.

That meant taking the "fleshy part" of the hedge apple and doing my "chemistry" thing by massacring a batch and taking extractions with ethanol and water. We did that by running extracts down the "specialized sand" to assess various compounds present from: 1) the fruity pulp (where there was virtually zero nutrition); 2) the pulp itself, with four key elements in the mature state that were measured against anti-inflammatory, anti-viral, anti-bacterial and anti-fungal potentials (where we would need to increase the potency to 10 times that of aspirin). Nothing much there either.

That took us to what amounted to the complete examination of everything in the hedge apples, except the seeds.

The one report I had read that made sense was one from Israel in 2002 that mentioned using "oils" from the hedge balls. But after breaking down every imaginable compound I had to believe the oil that was referenced in the Israeli findings could not have come from the flesh of the hedge apples. So once again, all logic began to point to the seeds as containing the "an active ingredient" in the oils. The thought was the oil would carry the pharmacologically active compounds to the skin. Although the oil was known, no one made the leap of logic to examine it for the presence of bioactives and use it to deliver those bioactives. That was the proverbial tipping point where my hypothesis could turn into an attractive theory for this oil.

RJA: *Did you ever have any doubts along the way? Did fear ever strike a chord in you that asked that deadly question: Is this all going to be a waste of time?*

Todd: It's always a part of the scientific mindset to question and challenge. And it's certainly true that 95% of everything we try in the labs meets with failure. By the same token, that failure eliminates the impostors and gets you closer to the truth. So, even though I questioned, I was also becoming increasingly certain that whatever "treasure" came out of the Pomifera was going to come from the seeds.

I also had the powers of observation on my side. That's because over the years I had noted the feeding habits of squirrels, deer and raccoons that they always seemed to dig through the pulp to feed on the seeds. So that is where I came to be convinced that the true nutritional value in the hedge apple had to reside—from the seeds...and the oil that came out of them.

Whatever the underlying reasons I do know this much: Everything I had learned in the labs came up to this point. Even though I was pretty certain where the oil would be most prolific, I had to apply all my skills in the lab to confirm and refine my suspicions.

By now drawing the right kind of extractions was very much like being a code-breaker or a translator of ancient texts.

Refined formulations are almost always highly technical. And unless you had a PhD in Chemistry there was a good chance you wouldn't be able to extract anything from the studies. (And even if you had been lucky enough to stumble onto the results, you would never be able to articulate the pharmacological models in a way that would get them accepted by the FDA.)

That's when I had that double Eureka!* This was meant to happen. First, my Uncle Don had been the special cosmic messenger all these years. And his message had stayed with me. The seed, in every sense of the word, had been planted. Second, all my research in the chemistry labs, and all my varied job functions at Monsanto, Metaphore, Cambrex, Kempharm and ABC had prepared me to seek and extract this Pomifera oil and refine the formulation that would render it commercially viable. So I took about two pounds of hedge apples, chopped them up, carefully picked out the seeds with tweezers, washed the seeds with

---

* Eureka! The Greek word, meaning "I have found it." It was first declared by the scientist Archimedes upon discovering the axiom of displacement.

water, air dried then ground the seeds in a coffee grinder, and extracted the oil from the seeds via solvent extraction and then separated the oil from the solvent. Standard stuff.

Following up, I used some very well defined methodologies to address the cause and effect concepts. And then shortly a beautiful thing occurred: we had an oil that looked great, smelled awful, but felt wonderful on Susan's skin. Susan, God bless her, was the original Pomifera® Oil guinea pig.

RJA: *How did it make you feel when you realized that you had a winner? Or did that come later?*

Todd: I have to admit there is that rush you get in the beginning when you know you're onto something. Still I had to try a little focus group in my immediate circle. So I convinced Susan to try the original isolate of Pomifera Oil, and she thought it was terrific! Terrific indeed but also something that smelled really "earthy."

Even though she always has my back, Susan is a true professional and not the cheerleader type. So if anyone would have given me candid feedback, no holds barred, it would have been she.

RJA: *So, surely you followed up with more applications and more focus groups.*

Todd: Certainly. And we put out more samples and spread out our applications. Even in my initial probes, I was starting to learn that it was showing some phenomenal results for conditions like eczema, psoriasis, rashes, acne and dermatitis.

And this was some aspect of field-testing I could do as a PhD in Chemistry that I never would have had the credibility for had I just been another "guy" with a product. Also my clinical experience and toxicology filings with the FDA made be very credible with respect to what Pomifera® Oil may do and definitely what it couldn't.

But just as I was getting this kind of exceptional feedback for the Pomifera® Oil, I had to come to that crossroads where we either went for an ethical drug application—a category that would include running the gauntlet of FDA approvals, classifications, and very expensive testing. Or...we could use this as a natural oil that would be good for the skin and hair, and simply let the product speak for itself.

At the time we were initially testing and exploring the possibilities of our Pomifera® Oil, one of the hot new products sweeping through the world of personal care was something called Moroccanoil®. Moroccanoil® was made from the kernels of something called the Argan-tree that grows in Northern Africa (primarily Morocco). And several companies came out in the media offering a line of products (primarily) for hair. It was really nothing special, but the personal care market has always been drawn to the "next big thing." Especially if it is a new product category, which Moroccanoil® was perceived to have created. Whether it was accurate or not, the companies were masterful in their marketing of this new oil—as if it were some ancient secret from a mystical land far away. Whatever the hype, the image was sufficiently exotic to attract a market that literally exploded overnight.

Now, there are good many useless "oils" out there that were long on promise and short on delivery. And even with viable compounds like Aloe Vera, there are so many knock-off and watered down versions, that all most people are doing is trading on a "name."

One thing we decided early on: we didn't want to be like those guys. We actually wanted to bring an original to market… with viable, credible genuine benefits.

By the same token, I didn't want to be another Dr. Oz and be pimping for every new "natural" product coming down the pike. That way you start out with some credibility but lose it quickly by making too many claims that, at best, just can't be met and (at worst) might get you into trouble with oversight groups like the FDA.

RJA: *So, early on you came to a kind of crossroads here, I would have to imagine. Do you go for an ethical drug and all the perils you had faced when you were at ABC, KemPharm and Metaphore? Or do you bring your scientific expertise into the realm of "natural products?"*

Todd: Exactly. In a way it always comes down to the Western Medicine approach to the market, or the Eastern Medicine approach to the market. Western medicine has very well defined methodologies to address cause and effect relationships. It works from symptomology, and paradigms of diagnosis/prognosis. But any way you look at it, the process is grueling and very expensive. And once you isolate and get the right model you still may spend years in test before you can get it out to the public.

The Eastern approach to natural remedies says something like "Here is our oil, extract, or herb. We make no claims. But let's try it and see if you feel better." You invoke the principles of trial and error, without overextending yourself with claims. Still all the while being mindful that we needed to be sure that it was being used in a safe manner. It entails more of a risk taker mentality, because the marketplace is replete with natural products that don't work. However, I felt that if I could use my Western Medicine street cred to openly and honestly bridge to the Eastern Medicine crowd we could stand out from the noise. Of course, Pomifera® Oil needed to perform along the way.

But in a way you are trusting in the power of Nature to find its own level, and you're trusting your product to merge with its own destiny. At best all you can do is be the right kind of agent for that to take place. And of course that sounds much easier than it is.

RJA: *So from what I can gather, and all that I have seen up to now, this is the path you decided to take.*

Todd: Yes it is. So… we were on our way to finalizing our product model. Now we had to develop our business model. And that would take some doing.

That's because we were going from the laboratory where we felt on solid ground into areas where there still remained so much to be learned. And did we ever learn…sometimes the hard way. (Talk about "kissing frogs!" My lips should have warts.)

RJA: *And at the risk of making assumptions, I will "deduce" that this is where we will pick up on the rest of this leg of the journey.*

Todd: Yes, we will.

(**Note:** At this point, I note with some irony that we all know how this story ends—happily at least to this point. What I find absolutely fascinating is the fact that there have been so many times along the way that it could have easily ended in disaster. Then again, that's what makes this adventure as fascinating as it is—the little dash of uncertainty that always spices the broth.)

"Todd and I work well together. We balance each other. He is bold and adventurous. He is the eternal optimist. I, on the other hand, am the ultimate skeptic. Originally I admit I had my concerns about Pomifera, but when I saw how much it was able to help people, I knew we couldn't go wrong with that...I'm still really amazed at how things have come together so completely, and as quickly they have."

*~ **Susan Johnson***

CHAPTER 9

BUSINESS MODELS
AND BURIED TREASURE

"The hardest thing to explain is the glaringly evident,
which everybody has decided not to see."

~ Ayn Rand, The Fountainhead

Todd Johnson is a fascinating study on occasion, because there are times that make him seem like a living contradiction when he is almost entirely consistent in everything he does. One of his favorite books is Ayn Rand's *The Fountainhead.* His personal hero is the genius inventor Nikola Tesla. And his favorite film is *It's A Wonderful Life.*

All three seem to bring entirely different issues to the fore when in fact they are all strikingly familiar in that they all feature courageous men who overcome tremendous odds to accomplish great things in their lives. In *The Fountainhead,* Howard Rourke is an architect before his time who faces constant assaults against his prodigious talent along with attempts to compromise his creations, but rises to the top of his profession in spite of them. Nikola Tesla, the man who brought us safe usable electricity, was the most pirated inventor of all time, and yet his genius changed the world. And in Frank Capra's *It's A Wonderful Life,* George Bailey (played by Jimmy Stewart) is that everyman who risks everything he has to lift his town out from under the yoke of a ruthless financier. Swindled and depressed he is convinced his life has been without value and decides to end it, until a guardian angel shows him that he has always been everybody's hero.

I mention these parallels to Todd, and he thinks about it for a moment. "Yeah, come to think of it, you're right. Well, I think we need more good guys. That's for sure.

"Anyway, I've always been a firm believer in reading about something, learning everything you can and then taking a deep dive into people who actually know how to make things happen... and who know things I don't."

I don't need to ask if he thinks he's one of those people. At this point we're past rhetorical questions. Still, I start this conversation with what probably amounts to another.

RJA: *I have to ask you: The last time we left off you had taken that quantum leap of faith, not only with Pomifera oil, but also with the decision to go with what was a 100% natural product. And you did so knowing that it had some pretty powerful potentials to be the next topical miracle potion. Didn't you ever have any doubts?*

Todd: There is always that hard-science mentality that wants to push the limits of efficacy. But in this case, my natural instincts took hold in every sense of the word. From everything I discovered in my experiments, Pomifera® Oil has proved to be one of the most bioactive products in Nature.

It is 100% natural and it turns out it is extremely stable. That meant it could easily be cold pressed and still maintain its purity without any need for chemical additives to preserve its long-term integrity. It seems to help remediate the impact of being in the sun too long. Paradoxically, according to the FDA testing parameters for what is identified as a *Sun Protection Factor,* Pomifera® Oil has an SPF of zero! So clearly we cannot claim any SPF value or that it is an SPF product. That means, as far as institutional measures are concerned, One Drop Wonder™ and Pomifera® Oil have an SPF of zero for now and eternity. Still it is a darn good thing to put on your skin before and after going out in to the sun!

RJA: *Wow! That is unusual. Even top quality Aloe Vera has to have something like* Potassium sorbate *to trim the enzymatic activity so it doesn't spoil on the shelves. So you can say... 100% Pure for Pomifera and actually mean it.*

Todd: I was even more encouraged by the fact that in peer review studies some of the compounds present in Pomifera® Oil had already shown some anti-microbial qualities similar to penicillin, and anti-inflammatory aspects that were better than most analgesics.

The beauty of Pomifera is that the molecules that comprise the oil are very small. That makes them appear to be able to penetrate deep into skin tissue. The molecular weight is unique because it appears to penetrate deeply into the epidermis (or outer layer of skin). By all indications, it also appears that the oil is getting into the dermis. That way it moisturizes in an extraordinary way. So the combination of the macro properties of the oil, with the bioactives in the oil, appear to stimulate collagen growth. That results in thousands of testimonies for fewer wrinkles and less inflammatory damage, and without any apparent accompanying toxicity. It appears to be very non-invasive.

From all the feedback we were getting from our customers, Pomifera® Oil was also turning out to be effective against things like athlete's foot fungus, and is also able to soothe burns like sunburn without a lot of peeling. It is looking to be antifungal and antiseptic as well. So it was the complete package. It is fantastic for amelioration of scars (new and old), filling in fine lines and wrinkles, and soothing anything that is red, angry, chafed or scraped.

Add to that the fact that it seems to have a very low incidence of allergic reaction (I have to believe that's because it is both non-GMO and a seed oil). By now, we've had hundreds of thousands of applications and only a handful of reported allergic reactions. (Of course, if you have a "seed oil" allergy issue you might want to consult a health professional before you use it.)

Still, the oil itself has such remarkable qualities, some masseuses use it as a carrying agent in their massage therapy sessions. And the oil itself softens and repairs tissue in ways that are actually visible to the naked eye.

RJA: *That's a pretty potent combination. I mean, however anecdotal the feedback might be, it still had to be the most encouraging news you could have wanted.*

Todd: And that's the point, isn't it. It was great to get all these reports about the Pomifera® oil. But it was strictly from personal experience and not the result of any clinical trials. So we had to go back to that original crossroads and decide. Do we plunge into some clinical trials and try to fall under the scrutiny of the FDA? Or do we launch this as a natural wonder and let word of mouth carry the weight. Let the oil speak for itself rather than have me do all of the talking.

That also meant we as a company couldn't, and shouldn't, make any medical claims because that would "red flag" our product virtually out of the gate.

RJA: *So… you went the other way. Or so it seems.*

Todd: Perhaps a little too far the other way, as we eventually came to find out. Understand that by now we were well into 2013 by the time we got all the research underway. So we made our evaluations and decided to define our original product approach.

At this point, I have to emphasize that running clinical trials would always be something we were going to keep as a long-term

> *"There is always that hard-science mentality that wants to push the limits of discovery. But in this case, my natural instincts took hold in every sense of the word. From everything I discovered in my experiments, Pomifera Oil has proved to be one of the most bioactive products in Nature."*

option. But that was something now on a far horizon in another time and place.

For the time being, we decided to go with an all-natural product, skip any kind of clinical or animal testing (which I find flawed to begin with). And since we decided on that path, we earned a Leaping Bunny Certification, which meant we were one of the good guys and didn't do any animal testing.

RJA: *Yes, I was horrified to realize that about 80% of all cosmetic and personal care companies still do dermal testing and LD-50 (kill ratios) on animals when none of it is actually required by the Personal Care Products Council (PCPC).*

Todd: Well, most of the major players in the industry do it to keep their liability down, but most animal testing they conduct is really over the top. Lab testing on animals is so flawed anyway. 97.5% of all lab tests can be evaluated successfully *in vitro* (in petri-dishes or agar plates). And there are so many variables from one animal species to the next when you're testing for things like pH balance and allergies, the only accurate test animal should be the human being.

Frankly, I didn't want to start out this new company that way. And that's why we agreed to take the direction we did.

RJA: *So you played it safe and went to the personal care, hair care sector—shampoos, conditioners and hair treatments? What pushed you over there?*

Todd: I don't think anything could be classified as "safe" in those early days. We thought we could create the best product family in a high demand market while we were still learning how to run all the traps for harvesting, manufacture and production…and then we still had to create a business model in a niche market—primarily hair care, shampoos and conditioners in what was a highly saturated market.

RJA: *I actually want to cover the production and manufacture of Pomifera Oil a little later, because that is a whole story on its own. For now, though, I have to assume you got it together enough to have some kind of product ready for market by 2014. And you had a product already proven effective in so many aspects of skin care, and yet you went full bore into hair care. Was it the path of least resistance?*

Todd: No. It's what initial product demand told us was the warmest market. It was an easy sell. By that point, we were in the process of putting together our business model. And we had retained a "high profile" marketing firm that we paid $100 K to get us a foothold in the retail marketplace.

RJA: *Uh oh! I think I know where this is headed. Don't tell me, they promised the penthouse and gave you the outhouse.*

Todd: Well, let me put it this way… We were a lot better at setting up a research model and product model than we were at creating an effective business and distribution model. Realizing that we might need some help in that area, we retained the services of some highly recommended advertising and marketing "hotshots" to help us do it. And wow! Did that ever turn out to be a wrong move…or in this case, series of moves.

In all fairness to our decision-making at the time, these guys brought all the right credentials—the highly touted track-record and all the bells and whistles. But in hindsight, I wonder if they were representing themselves with absolute integrity, because everything—and I mean everything—they recommended turned out to be absolute garbage. To top it off, they didn't execute it particularly well; in fact it was all lousy.

The packaging was all wrong, the website was a flop, their internet strategy was a disaster, and they were trying to force the matrix in a personal care marketplace where major hair care giants like Redken, Matrix, Moroccanoil, and Paul Mitchell have annual ad budgets of millions of dollars. So we didn't stand a chance.

RJA: *Believe me, you're not the first startup company to be seduced by the mavens of Madison Avenue. I'm sure you realized sooner rather than later that you had to cut your losses. So when did you drop the dime on these guys?*

Todd: I'm not sure it's much consolation to know there are other fools out there. But, I do remember when we started, because the pain is emblazoned in my memory. Originally, we got sucked into the dog and pony show around January of 2014. And it took us until August to scrap the whole campaign and flush these so-called "experts" along with it.

RJA: *All right. So now you've got a very solid shampoo and hair care product and (to a lesser extent) a natural oil for topical use. So...how did you shake off your losses and rebound?*

Todd: It wasn't easy, I can tell you. We had already had some success with aestheticians and salons. So I decided to become salon-centric in our approach to sales.

I stress here that Erik is remaining my silent partner in this. So I'm taking all the bruising and setbacks directly on the chin. (I mean he's hurting along with me, but he's still CEO of Tjaden Biosciences. And I'm the one in the trenches. In this case, "the trenches" entailed literally loading up the trunk of my car with product and taking my show on the road.)

RJA: *Well, don't feel too bad. Success guru Wayne Dyer, Mary Kay Ash, and Alfred Carl Fuller (of Fuller Brush fame) all built their businesses this way.*

Todd: Yes, but this is the age of the Internet, and here I was actually compelled to use some very old technology just to keep the doors open. Top that off by the fact that this all started right around my 50th birthday.

So, here I am hitting a mid-life crisis accentuated by the fact that I'm a Chemistry PhD and former science rockstar reduced to door-to-door salon sales in Iowa, Nebraska and some parts of South Dakota.

Talk about a humbling experience! I was having one. And I have to say it was all I could do to keep my spirits up. The one salvation was that my efforts were at least keeping us cash-flow neutral. Thankfully the samples I was giving out of the Pomifera® Oil were winning converts all over the place. And I managed to keep faith with my intention—that was always there.

RJA: *Then you were, consciously or unconsciously, planting seeds for Pomifera Oil all over the Midwest. (Yes! I confess to the pun.)*

Todd: Oh, very consciously! If there is one thing I am it's persistent. And things like doubt and self-pity are only useful if they motivate you to do something. So I was motivated. I believed in the potential. I tilled my "Field of Dreams." And what is it they say in the story? "If you build it, they will come."

RJA: *In this case, they did come. Or in this case, she did. I'm talking about one time noted "beauty blogger" and YouTube interviewer, Kendra Aarhus.*

Todd: Kendra certainly made a difference. I think in every success story there are those special people who come along—those messengers who help take you to the next level. She certainly turned out to be that person for Pomifera® Oil. And since I've always believed in destiny and divine right order, this all couldn't have come at a more opportune time.

RJA: *But I believe you told me this it didn't happen overnight. So… could you sort of give a brief chronology?*

Todd: Sure! But to do that, let's backtrack to that little point of critical mass in my life—August of 2014 and my 50th birthday. Because by that time I'd really hit a low point. In fact, on that particular day, I had been writing orders at $150 a pop. And I went to pick up my daughter Emily at the University of Iowa and remember feeling this crushing sense of futility and thinking: *I'm 50 years-old, and where am I in my life? What have I done? What am I doing?*

Literally after we got home, I had to go into my bedroom, get down on my knees, humble myself and ask for guidance. Not surprisingly, shortly after I did that I was infused with what at the time seemed and inexplicable sense of wellbeing—a knowledge that things would start to turn.

Then about a week later, I got a call from a salon franchise called Cost Cutters owned by Evans Enterprises with an order to put our Pomifera Hair Care products into their Salons.

The salons took the product but kept using our oil. The lady who gave us our first break in the hair care space was Evans Enterprises CEO Joni Evans. That relationship was certainly rewarding. But what was even more significant was something that it led to a couple of months later. That's when Joni introduced me to a gentleman named Chris Feigen. Chris ran a number of beauty colleges under the banner of Capri College. And when he took the line, he in turn introduced me to a beauty blogger and dynamo named Kendra Aarhus, which turned out not to be as easy as you might imagine.

RJA: *Actually, I can imagine. Because I recently interviewed Kendra, who told me the whole story from her perspective. Great copy!*

Todd: …Which I'm sure you will be dropping in this document shortly. And yes! Originally she was a tough interview, because she was at a place in her life when she was phasing out of this sort of thing. So she actually blew off our first meeting because, in her words "She didn't need to look at another hair care line."

Well, you know me by now. So that just made me more determined to get my story in front of her, especially when I found out that Kendra had about 2 million people making weekly hits on her beauty blog for About.com. From what I learned about her, Kendra Aarhus had integrity, credibility and quite a following—all three qualities I knew would make a difference for Pomifera should she decide to become an advocate.

Understand, this all didn't just happen overnight. By now, it was around March or April of 2015, and we'd been working to get Pomifera up to the next level and having a pretty difficult time of it. I was still feeling my way around with our hair care products in the marketplace. So this, to me, was the kind of opportunity we needed.

Long story short, Chris ended up finally convincing Kendra to take a meeting. She was skeptical at first, but I gave her several product samples of both the shampoo and hair products and the Pomifera® Oil for skin care. Kendra took the products with her, tried them out, and it didn't take long for her to catch on to the fact that our products were something special—especially the Pomifera® Oil.

In fact, Kendra was the very first person to drop the hammer down on me and practically insist that we needed to make a serious "skin care" product out of Pomifera® Oil.

I think she said something like, "This oil is incredible! You need to need to make this your main product, and you need to do it like immediately." And to our utter delight, she followed up by giving us a terrific review in her next blog, which turned out to be a boon for Pomifera Hair Care.

RJA: *Kind of a Tipping Point I suppose? Or at least the beginning of one. I guess, though, she had one last gesture that proved even more of a door-opener for you.*

Todd: Yes, one thing I came quickly to value in Kendra is the fact that she never committed to something she didn't absolutely believe in. So, I was honored by her endorsement. I was also intrigued by the fact that she personally decided to shift her career emphasis to become one of the first big Founder-Distributors (aka Beauty Guide) for a company called LimeLight by Alcone.

LimeLight by Alcone is currently becoming a very large Direct Sales personal care company with about 20,000 distributors worldwide and a terrific reputation for having products that were a way ahead of the curve.

According to Kendra, she was attending a gathering of leading distributors in Chicago, and actually taking a private meeting with LimeLight by Alcone's CEO, a woman named Michele Gay. So apparently, she gets into the car with Michele with a whole pitch prepared.

By reputation, Michele is a very "New York" kind of woman, and is not inclined to beat around the bush. So her first question was, "So what is going on that I don't know about?" Kendra's response was equally direct and to the point, and went something like: "I've met this mad scientist in Southern Iowa who has this amazing skin-care product called Pomifera Oil…"

Whatever she followed up with must have worked because I shortly got a phone call from Michele who tells me, "Kendra thinks I should talk to you about this oil. I get about 10 in calls a day and only make about 2 outside calls a year. You have just become 1 of my 2, so tell me what's going on."

So, here's the point of irony in all this, because Kendra neglected to fill me in on the full context of her meeting with Michele. So my response, flat-footed as it caught me, was "Well you have my attention, because you want to know about my oil. So I am thrilled to have this call…"

Of course, I would have been a lot more reverential had I known who this woman actually was. But as it turned out things probably worked in my favor because I wasn't as impressed as I definitely should have been. So she took me as someone who had been around the block a time or two.

The better news was that Michele Gay eventually became impressed with the Pomifera® Oil samples I sent her. She fanned out bottles to a half-dozen of her key people and the feedback she got more or less blew her away.

After that, she sent out about 40 more units to her next level of major players at LimeLight's 2015 Summit Meeting and once again she got hit with what were described to me as "overwhelmingly positive results." Apparently this was unheard of at the time to make such an immediate positive impression. And in November of 2015, we received our first major order with LimeLight, and that's how a product called "One Drop Wonder™" was born. It's certainly our flagship product now with hundreds of thousands of bottles in circulation.

At least that's the shorthand version. The full texture of the story of course is much more richly woven.

RJA: *The product name,* One Drop Wonder™, *says it all. I mean a little bit goes a long way. But in a way that usually goes against the grain of all the tenets of product consumption. We tend to want to encourage people to use a lot of something…and slather it on to encourage frequency of product use.*

Todd: That works, I suppose, if you have no concern about personal credibility and product integrity. The fact is that the Pomifera® Oil is hard to come by in that we have to work so very hard to separate the seeds from the pulp of the hedge apple. The absolute truth is that the oil is quite expensive to process and manufacture. So, it's pretty pricey at any level. The other part of that equation is that it truly does so much with so little—it is so deeply penetrative and so broad-spectrum in its benefits—that this too becomes part of its well-earned reputation for healing and all those intangibles that make it one-of-a-kind.

RJA: *I know you get a lot of praise for having researched, perfected and created this phenomenal product. Do you feel that certain rush of creation—a godlike power if you will—for having brought something like this to life? I mean, you are effectively acknowledged as the "inventor" of Pomifera oil.*

Todd: Well, that's just it. I didn't. It was always there in Nature— a part of God's Pharmacy. As we know by now there are nearly 400,000 different plant species in the world. And if you believe as Einstein did that, "God doesn't play dice with the universe," then you have to believe most of them have a purpose—a very high purpose in the case of Pomifera Oil.

Its intrinsic qualities have always been there like buried treasure. All I did was take the broken fragments of the treasure map and glue them back together. That's how great discoveries are made.

So perhaps words like "inventor" or "creator" really don't fit me. I'm an explorer in the endless terrain of the biochemical continent. So maybe I'm more like Indiana Jones than DaVinci.

RJA: *Either way, that's pretty lofty company you're keeping.*

Todd: Yeah, well… I've also been lucky. And that has made all the difference.

RJA: *I'm also a big believer that "good luck" follows industrious people. And the better news for Pomifera® Oil is that this is not the beginning of the end, but the end of the beginning. This is where the story really gets interesting.*

Todd: Well, I agree. This was the breakthrough. The last six months of 2015 were where we really started to turn the corner. It's hard to believe that was only a couple of years ago that we signed our exclusive agreement with LimeLight by Alcone. And yes! All the best news and some of the best parts of the story are yet to come.

AN INTERVIEW WITH KENDRA AARHUS

It's a funny thing about my career as a beauty blogger and that unexpected inter- section with Todd Johnson. Because, it was about that time in 2015 that I decided I was pretty much finished with that part of my professional journey. Despite hav- ing had a respectable following, I was hitting a crisis of consciousness in that I never wanted to use my blog as a negative platform to ruin a company's future. And at the time I was getting hit with a lot of substandard prod- ucts that I just couldn't in good conscience endorse.

So when I got a phone call from Chris Feigan at Capri College about some "shampoo made from hedge apples," my first reaction was that it had to be maybe the dumbest idea I had ever heard. (And I "just knew" I wouldn't like them.) I didn't want to give another bad review, so I just decided to avoid the whole thing and cancelled the first interview.

But, as I soon found out, Todd Johnson is both per- sistent and passionate about his product. And after meeting with him for about 15 minutes, I could see that this product was something very special. I also realized that the real value in the Pomifera oil was not going to be in their hair products at all but in all the incredible things it did for the skin. So, my contribution for Todd and Pomifera and LimeLight, I guess was three-fold.

First, I was able to quickly convince Todd to double down on the superior qualities of this incredible oil and all it could do for the skin. Shortly after, the article about Pomifera Hair Care was posted on my website, he was starting to get quite a few orders.

The second thing I was able to do was to get the whole product line in front of Michele Gay, the CEO at LimeLight, and convince her to take a serious look at Pomifera and "this mad scientist in Iowa who is making 'champagne' out of hedge apples." Michele is a smart woman and saw the concept in a bigger picture than I ever did. She and her core group immediately fell in love with the Pomifera Oil and decided to introduce it to the field during their New York City Sales Summit in June 2015.

So, I guess the third thing I did while listening to the initial concepts was speak loudly about what a phenomenal product this group of 40 initial test subjects had in their hands. I became an ambassador for the possibilities, and everyone was thrilled. After that, they ended up calling it *One Drop Wonder*™. I know Todd gives me a lot of credit. But I think he gives me too much praise. Some things are just meant to happen. *Pomifera* would have taken off anyway. Maybe I just helped speed up the process.

CHAPTER 10

NUTS AND BOLTS, APPLES AND ORANGES: ALL THE STUFF OF DREAMS

"In Nature there is no such thing as waste.
In Nature…everything is recycled."

~ David Suzuki, PhD/Canadian Broadcaster

It just occurred to me that, as an industry, the product Pomifera® Oil (aka One Drop Wonder™)generates a negative carbon footprint. Practically no one else, except a few solar companies and some "environmental architects" who design zero energy homes can make that claim.

Todd Johnson and Osage Healthcare, Inc. can. In fact, it's a point of pride with him, and why wouldn't it be? Pomifera now annually takes one of Mother Nature's "junk plants" and gives it a meaning, a purpose and a reputation for being one of the biggest natural product surprises of the last 20 years. As such the company harvests several hundred tons of hedge apples that would otherwise either be cast off or kicked into ditches or left to rot as a kind of ecological nuisance and arboreal "weed."

Now, farmers and ranchers who previously had to spend money to clear them out, or simply try to gutter them to get them out of the way have economic access to providing a new kind of "cash crop." And this has become a turnaround story all its own.

As we close on that tipping point where Pomifera® Oil crosses over from a product wallflower to that "secret sauce that helps promote both beauty and healing" we have to note the irony with a sense of satisfaction that is unique. Now Pomifera® Oil is rapidly becoming everyone's object of desire. Now it is the next big thing, in fact. With that in mind, I have to hit Todd with how it feels to be that unexpected creator of a whole new industry in the American heartland. And that begins our next conversation:

RJA: *So… have you now officially rescued Pomifera and the Osage Orange from the scrapheap of history?*

Todd: Ha ha! Well, that's funny but not entirely accurate. I mean, they were quite the delicacy to the Wooly Mammoth back in the Pleistocene Era about 400,000 years ago. And even now, they're finding possible uses for hedge apples as an insect repellent and insectostatic agent…to get rid of everything from spiders to cockroaches. So who knows? As science finds that crack in the door, we may be entering a virtual "gold rush" period for hedge apples.

RJA: *Much thanks to you, it seems. I mean, here you are: not only a new industry in Southern Iowa, but also one that has taken a blight, an ecological burden that people actually have to clear away, and*

now farmers are harvesting the stuff and getting paid for it…by you! How does that make you feel?

Todd: It feels pretty good. We ran some numbers a few months ago and determined that our current demands for hedge apples—outside our own manufacturing—have generated an estimated $300,000 in additional income for local farmers and non-profit organizations and provided at least full to part-time work for about 6 people (outside of the ten or so we employ directly). So, literally in this case, one person's trash has become another person's treasure.

RJA: *But you've just reached this point, recently.*

Todd: In the last couple of years, yes! I think the fact that the "One Drop Wonder™" has taken off so well with LimeLight by Alcone, and the fact that LimeLight has become such an incredible force for good in making us semi-famous has had its own trickle down effect on all the local economies…and on us directly of course.

RJA: *And you are now approaching or surpassing that coveted seven-digit crossover for revenues, which means you are running a very efficient cost-to-profit ratio for Pomifera.*

Todd: True. And that's the point, isn't it? Lean and (not so) mean.

RJA: *I do want to cover your having crossed over that very fascinating consumer threshold with you because that's where we bring in so many new players and your support role in the red-hot field of direct* sales. But for the time being, I'd like to know more about how you actually managed to pull all this together.

Todd: Well, let me take you back to that pivotal point after the summer of 2015. I remember it well, because it was in September right after LimeLight's Summit Meeting that they officially gave our product the Greenlight to go ahead with manufacturing and distribution.

The first orders came in and they were surprising, because they not only embraced our Pomifera® Oil (now officially One Drop Wonder™) as their only exclusive product, they also wanted to possibly look at current and future Pomifera® brand products.

I have to admit that I was a bit surprised at the level of commitment and enthusiasm LimeLight showed for Pomifera virtually from the start of things. But I don't think I was quite prepared to expect the kind of marketing genius that Michele Gay and her niece Madison Mallardi brought to the table. As it turned out, they knew exactly what to do with our product and how to give it the level of exposure it needed to put it over with their people in the field.

The rest the product did for itself. As you know, you can only have so much "buzz" about a product. And when it hits, you'd better have something that can deliver on promise or else you're DOA in a very short time. The good news for us is that One Drop Wonder™ seldom fails to deliver on promise…and then some. We immediately knew we had a winner.

So it only followed the logical upward curve that came for us in the next year was a period of exponential growth and along with it a ramped up demand that we had to be ready for.

RJA: *Knowing you, I can't imagine that you wouldn't be prepared for such a time. And I had to believe you had the technology in place to meet the demand.*

Todd: Yes, we'd gotten on top of that issue for the most part. But not even I was entirely ready for what was coming next. It started with a slow curve followed by a deluge. And it was absolutely all we could do to meet the need.

RJA: *But apparently you did, because I note that you're still here and quite capable of coping with what seems to have become a windfall. What fascinates me is the fact that, there is no manufacturing technology I know of that is specifically designed to break down hedge apples, separate the seeds from them and then cold press the seeds into a viable family of products. So, how did you do it?*

Todd: Well, that's where we start this anchor leg of the journey. Because no matter how prepared you think you are there is a learning process, and there are growing pains. And as necessity truly is the mother of invention, I had to put on my inventor's hat early in the game.

RJA: *Seems to me to be very complex indeed. How did you manage? If I know anything about extraction, compression and processing, you had to have about five machines to do all this. And I'm guessing you weren't prepared for mass production.*

Todd: You'd be guessing correctly. But then, that's when you learn to prize innovation above all other qualities. And I'm a firm believer in the fact that the right people will come up with the right solutions at the right time.

RJA: *Did you ever feel the pressure would be too much? Did you ever feel overwhelmed? (It would only be natural if you did.)*

Todd: Well there are two ways to look at pressure. You can let it break you…and break you down. Or you can believe as I do that pressure is what makes diamonds. So, if anything, I think life is a diamond mine!

I do have to admit that once we got the exclusive agreement with LimeLight for One Drop Wonder™, I felt both a great sense of relief followed by one of challenge.

One thing that made me aware of the necessity to do it right was the faith that LimeLight and Michele Gay had placed in me and in the product. I'm sure, like most smart professionals, she had vetted me to some degree. But from that time in 2015 up until the following LimeLight Palooza in Orlando in 2016, we never actually met face to face. So this relationship was one of professional trust.

RJA: *So from this point, September of 2015 going forward, you are facing a pretty massive production uptick. So, how did you handle it? That was more than your fair share of new machinery to work with. And I would imagine it had never been tested to that degree.*

Todd: The good news is that the "nuts and bolts" of our marketing was now being handled by the wonderful field people of LimeLight through their independent distributors (aka Beauty Guides) and their passion for networking an offering of natural, professional quality skincare and cosmetics. So we could concentrate on what we were prepared to do: making it happen at a production level. And I was ready for that.

RJA: *So, let's get down to the nuts and bolts of how you managed to process a product for which there had never been a production precedent. What were the ABCs of processing Pomifera Oil out of Nature and making it into a viable product?*

Todd: Well I have to say that I was inspired by Leonardo Da Vinci at some point, because if you study this man for more than five minutes you realize that he was undaunted in everything that faced him. He looked upon invention as the greatest challenge to his genius. And finding solutions always became his greatest adventure.

So…to invent and set up the right kind of equipment I had to use some innovation that required a blend some Leonardo bravado, a good bit of Monsanto technology, some things learned in the chemistry lab, and some good old Southern Iowa trailer park engineering that I actually recruited my dad to help me put together.

And the good news is that it all worked.

Realistically, creating or adapting new machines to produce a product are just adventures in problem solving. So getting hedge apples from harvest to packaged product all reduces down to finding the right machines for the job: some that already exist and some you just have to invent or cobble together.

The first one I came up with is what we call "the machine that goes 'Ping!'"

RJA: *Sounds like something out of Monty Python.*

Todd: Kind of looks like it too. It's basically what is called a Hammer Mill. And it's a piece of equipment from the 1950s where we feed frozen hedge apples into the machine to break them down.

(I have to note with some sense of irony that the first time we had to do this with any kind of mass basis was during the polar vortex that swept the Midwest in 2013-2014. And it was not much fun I can tell you. But believe me. Once you've successfully harvested, shipped, broken down and made Pomifera Oil during a Polar Vortex with minus 20 degree weather, everything else is a piece of cake!)

From there we had to get crushed hedge apples into what amounted to a basic tomato de-seeder to separate the valuable part of the pulp from the balls—the seeds—and that comes down more or less to applying an old gold mining strategy. That meant we used a dewatering screen and then passed a fan across them to get them to the first drying.

The second drying was even more bizarre on the surface of it, because we originally took the wet or damp seeds, bunched them up and threw them into a large clothes dryer.

RJA: *A large clothes dryer? Wow! And it worked!?*

Todd: A classic avocado colored clothes dryer (an antique) straight out of "That Seventies Show." But hey! It worked and worked well. And we kept it running full tilt from eight to ten hours a day. From there, we took the seeds from the dryer and poured them into a 5-gallon bucket. And we had it vented so that the seeds would fall in there so the dry seeds would not be able to tumble out (As a nice little tap on the wrist from Nature, we found the dry seeds would make a different sound when they fell. So in that strange but wonderful way, they more or less told us when they were ready.)

After we achieved the desired moisture content, we cold processed the seeds by crushing them. It was an innovation that came from our own invention and some tricks I'd learned from Mike Stern at Monsanto by applying the principles of variable design. From there, we got a laminate flow network of weirs to separate the solids from the liquids. And we applied that to a system that allowed us to maximize the oil.

By using this rather crude but very efficient method, we found we could process about a ton of hedge apples per day. However, in the very beginning we could only process 200 hedge apples a day. Leading me to question if I had made a disaster of a mistake to convince myself and Erik Tjaden that Pomifera® Oil was going to be the next big thing.

RJA: *A masterpiece of innovation. And I always admire that kind of ingenuity. But I had to bet you went through more than your fair share of trial and error, at least in the beginning.*

Todd: Oh, absolutely! But remember too that I come from the laboratory culture. Failure is just another rung on the ladder to achievement. And amazingly it worked! Some of it still does.

RJA: *Still, I've got to imagine that the added product demand would have overwhelmed that sooner rather than later. So…was there an angel in the woodpile? I'm guessing there was.*

Todd: Funny thing about success. It attracts solutions. And even though we got through part of 2015 at our originally established production rate, about that period of critical mass you mentioned, we were approached by a man in Pulaski, Iowa who had a design for the best hedgeball deseeder I had seen up to that point.

The machine cost about $20 K, and was probably the best contract arrangement I could imagine at the time. What he was able to do was use augurs in a "Bobcat" with a quarter ton bucket and drop them in a hopper. And he was able to separate and deliver the seeds on a massive level.

Knowing that, I pay him on a volume of delivered seeds, and we then operate a cold-pressing process here where we ultimately refine the oil.

We currently enjoy a long-term exclusive contract based on trust and mutual confidence in one another's abilities to deliver. So it's been a boon in all the very best ways.

We press the seeds and through a trade secret operation to create One Drop Wonder™ as an ecologically friendly, non-GMO, gluten-free, chemical-free pure vegan oil—one that's everything everyone wants from this kind of natural product.

RJA: *Sounds like the ideal arrangement. Have you thought about doing a manufacturing/processing video to tell the story?*

Todd: Eventually that might be on the menu. But for now, I have to admit we are ugly but efficient. Our goal is to produce a professional 2-4 minute video for LimeLight Palooza 2018. We have shot all the video and are now incorporating the audio/music to edit into a final product. The key to our success up to now has been learning to delegate...and trust. At this point, we are still enjoying the offshoots of a huge leap of faith, and up to now everything has worked.

RJA: *I know this probably sounds like nuts and bolts to some people, but I've always been fascinated about how things work. I think people in any business need to know that it isn't some little coterie of gnomes grinding on a mill wheel and stomping up and down in a wine press to get this stuff out.*

Todd: Well I suppose in a metaphorical sense you're not that far off. It is a kind of magical process that leads to an exceptional result. But in this case, the gnomes are just inventive hard-working Midwesterners. So that's a kind of magic all its own.

RJA: *Speaking of magic, ahem…let's get back to your rise to prestige and prominence with LimeLight and this whole new universe in which you find yourself. When did it all break open?*

Todd: That's a lot to gobble up in one sentence. It's really been a journey, and it's been gradual…until recently. Still, there have been milestones that have lent it a certain amount of drama, especially at LimeLight Palooza in 2016 when I met the first wave of LimeLight Beauty Guides.

Up to that point, my relationship with them had been pretty much one of blind faith. Michele Gay had placed a great deal of confidence in me, in Pomifera and in the whole One Drop Wonder™ product concept. My group and I had been fulfilling on time, delivering on promise while still remaining pretty much out of the loop of all the amazing reports that were starting to pour in about One Drop Wonder™.

Of course, we were getting feedback and reports from Lime-Light about all the great results their people were observing for all kinds of skin conditions—from very dramatic improvements in skin health and appearance of the users to curative reports for conditions like eczema and acne and even severely burned skin. A good many direct messages raved about our product as being "life-changing." They were all anecdotal of course, and I for one had to treat them as such. Nonetheless they seemed to rise in direct proportion to the volume of product orders that came cascading in.

So, by the time that LimeLight Palooza took place in August of 2016, I was now being requested to show up as a guest speaker.

So I prepared myself to do just that. What I wasn't prepared for was what would come next.

RJA: *So, what did come next? I mean here you show up at Lime-Light Palooza Orlando in 2016. And suddenly you are more or less a star of the show. You're actually raised to a rockstar status (yet again). You're the genius creator of this new first best hope of a product. But this time, were they confusing the message with the messenger?*

Todd: Well, it was quite a bit of culture shock in some very good ways. Because when I arrived, I finally got to meet and have dinner with Michele Gay, who turned out to be just as bright, dynamic and market savvy as I thought she would be.

Even then I believe she was trying to prepare me for what was to come, but I truly had no idea.

Understand, at this point, I had no real website to speak of, no media presence other than a couple of articles and a pair of YouTube interviews (one with Kendra Aarhus) and not that much public exposure. And yet from that smattering of information and public recognition, I was suddenly thrust into a throng of

400 "Beauty Guides" who were both enthusiastic and extremely impassioned to learn everything about Pomifera and about me.

Once I felt the full force of their support and passion for this "miracle" I had brought to their lives, I felt this wave of responsibility that I now had to be responsible for. And I had to bring all my credibility and professional chops to the table. After all, I had brought this revolutionary natural elixir for health and beauty that (according to them) was changing people's lives, and it was now incumbent upon me to take complete responsibility for it.

RJA: *In what ways? Was it oppressive, all this new attention? Or did you kind of enjoy it?*

Todd: Well, I'll give you a little episode when I first got to the LimeLight Palooza in 2016. I arrived at the Orlando Airport around 11 p.m. and I don't get to my hotel until around midnight. I book my room and am scrambling around trying to grab a bite to eat when I run into about 8 LimeLight "Beauty Guides," eating and partying, when they see me and cry out: "Are you Todd Johnson?"

When I acknowledge the obvious, they come over to me and (self-admittedly) start "fan-girling." (I didn't even know there was such a term, but apparently they did and even busted themselves for doing so.)

They were so pumped up and so motivated by their product experiences that they were dying to share them with me. Apparently our One Drop Wonder™ was changing their lives. And for a brief time with these six or eight women I *was* the product. And it was almost impossible to separate myself from it. So in that almost bizarre context it becomes almost impossible to separate truth from illusion.

So I am a "rockstar" sort of. But I'm also that science nerd who's kind of viewed as intimidating intellectually. So it's a very fine line to walk.

RJA: *So, how did you?*

Todd: On a very human level because, in the end, humanity trumps everything. And I caught onto the energy involved in a very healthy way. Since almost all actions are either a "you are a genius or an answered prayer," I saw all this as a humbling response by so many women that Pomifera® Oil was changing lives across such a broad spectrum of wonderfully thankful people. And I quickly caught on to the fact that this might be the first wave among many.

RJA: *So you actually regained your balance and planned your strategies from there? Or how did you plan to handle it?*

Todd: I think partly by just accepting what came next and embracing it. And it was not that hard because several things about this gathering caught my attention in a very short time.

I was immediately struck by the sincerity of these women. The energy, enthusiasm, passion, commitment and intelligence they displayed were pretty off the hook. These were real professionals who cared deeply about their business and about helping others. They wanted all the tools necessary to make that happen. And this had so obviously been part of what they had been looking for.

I was brought in as "the expert." So I was the source. And though they had already received advanced notice that I was "that mad scientist who had created all this," they were truly respectful and treated me with a kind of intellectual reverence I probably didn't deserve.

Well by now you know me. I'm pretty good at putting people at ease. I genuinely liked this new "family" of mine. And I loved their commitment to this. So I tried to make myself as available as possible and answer every one of the questions they had.

What I also realized at the time, that I was going to have to step up my game in terms of three things: 1) accessibility; 2) information and education; and 3) a viable media presence.

This was a real "aha" moment for me…and a wake-up call. I was going to have to be *visible, approachable and accountable.* My new job as the face of the One Drop Wonder™ franchise was to make myself available. That meant some new forays into Social

I think my father's attitude is the reason we are all where we are today. He has this terrific ability 24/7 to know what's important and what isn't. He also puts the best possible face on anything he does and dresses it in enthusiasm. I remember when he first started talking about hedge apples and Pomifera, my sister Emily and I both asked, "This isn't like fried cookie dough is it?" We were kidding, but he was serious. And aren't we all better off right now that he was…

~ Leah Johnson

Media like Facebook and Twitter. And believe me I was a stranger in that strange land.

RJA: *So you were learned in all the ways of science and technology but somewhat...backward in the ways of modern communication?*

Todd: "Backward" is such a harsh word. Let's just say I had a learning curve when it came to polishing my social media skills. And thank God I had two very smart, media savvy Millennial daughters who could help me break into that world and actually look like I knew what I was doing.

RJA: *So in the late summer of 2016, you got back and rebooted your entire media presence for Todd Johnson and Pomifera®. And since that time you have become a Facebook celebrity and social media maven. So has it made a difference?*

Todd: In more ways than I imagined...Since I took that bold plunge into that wonder-world of Facebook *et al,* I've become more visible. I'm more accessible. I'm more hands-on. And even better, I'm able to feel the pulse of all these great Beauty Guides and fans of all things Pomifera®. We communicate on a regular basis—sometimes weekly—and it's super for feedback. I have my hands on the pulse of what's going on in the field. I'm also able to do things like post mini webinars and promotional new use ideas to the Beauty Guides in the field. And I get to let people take an occasional inside look at what we're doing and how we're growing at Pomifera®.

RJA: *I know Susan is in the business with you and you refer to her as "The Lieutenant." Do your daughters, Emily and Leah, continue to help as well?*

Todd: Oh yes! For sure! Even though Emily is a practicing BSN/RN, and Leah is now in a pre-veterinary medicine program at Iowa State, they're always giving me input and ideas—sometimes great ones.

One of the important things I've learned from working with LimeLight is that, even though they love our product, everyone is always looking for the next big thing. Expanding product lines with exciting new product concepts is a lifeline for these companies. And perhaps not surprisingly the most daring, outrageous new product concept to come along was introduced to us by my daughter Leah. Bath Bombs!

RJA: *Bath bombs!?*

Todd: It's all the rage with Millennials and seemingly the rest of the world. And most of them are junk; just a bunch of fizz. BUT we have come up with a great new line of all natural, non-GMO, pure ingredient bath bombs made from Pomifera® Oil. I came up with the formulation and introduced them about a year ago inside the company, and everyone I showed it to thought it was a horrible idea.

Well, you know the old Walt Disney story by now.

RJA: *Yes, I do. Whenever Walt Disney came up with a new concept, he would try the idea out on about half a dozen people. And if they all hated it, he knew he was onto something.*

Todd: Exactly! Well, that's what I did. And everyone thought I was out of my mind. They were all convinced it would fail big time. Especially since I was taking product development advice from an 18-year-old daughter.

RJA: *So… did it? Did bath bombs bomb?*

Todd: Well… that makes a great starting point for the next chapter.

RJA: *Actually, it doesn't because you already tipped your hand when you said Leah had come up with a really "great idea."*

Todd: Well…Spoiler alert! The Pomifera Bath Bombs were introduced in June of 2017 and soon became one of Pomifera's best selling products. In a way that has become the bellwether for our new arc with LimeLight in the last 12 months.

Because right now we are on a roll. And nothing has underscored that better than the most recent LimeLight Palooza 2017 in Austin, Texas.

RJA: *So do we pick up from there?*

Todd: And so many other things as well.

Note: it is here that I believe that Lao Tzu was right and that one picture is worth ten thousand words. So I attach a photo of Todd Johnson with his end stage refined Pomifera® Oil (the source of One Drop Wonder™). It is a beauty shot and the end result of about seven steps to get here. It's a part of my belief that every story deserves a happy-ending. And in a very product sense… this is it!

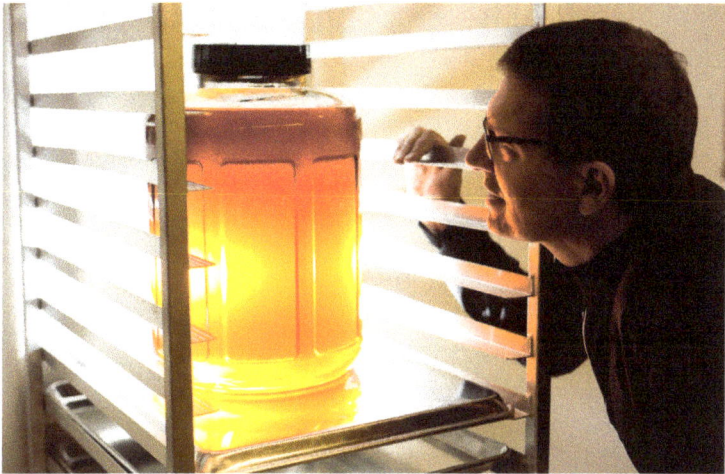

Todd Johnson quality checks a batch of finished refined Pomifera oil.

NATASHA RAMSEY: LIMELIGHT™

My experience with Pomifera oil was nothing short of phenomenal, and I'm excited to share it. Back in 2016, I was preparing some formula in my baby food blender when the blender exploded all over me, and I received some very serious second and third degree burns on my face, eyes, hands, neck and chest.

When I went to get the UCSD burn center to get my burns treated, the doctor who treated me predicted that (in his words) "There will be some scarring."

For my post trauma treatment I was supposed to scrub my face about five times a day and apply a regimen that included Polysporin®. It was about that time that a friend of mine had bought a bottle of One Drop Wonder™ and told me just how very effective in treating all kind of damage to the skin, including burns. So I decided to use it in my daily treatment regimen.

It meant that every day about five times a day I would scrub my face and then apply about 10 drops of the One Drop Wonder™ with the Polysporin®. And every time I did I could definitely feel a soothing effect on my skin.

I did that five times a day for about a month, and I was amazed at the results. (I was supposed to have a great deal of discoloration and could barely detect any.) After six months, I had virtually no scarring beyond one tiny spot on my neck.

Later I noticed that my husband's college friend was promoting LimeLight. And after I realized that One Drop Wonder™ was a major part of its product line, I knew this was something I would have to share.

Long story short, I was so passionate about sharing my experience so it could help others, I became a Lime-Light distributor and have been one ever since.

At this point, what's best about it is the good I'm able to do for others. In fact, even if I never got paid a penny for selling this, I still would, just knowing what One Drop Wonder™ can do for others. It is a labor of love. And I am a living testimony as to its effectiveness.

~ San Diego, California

ERIN JEANNE DOOHEN: LIMELIGHT™

M y story is deeply personal and comes with a happy-ending I would never have expected.

When I was five years old I was mauled by a dog. The trauma left scars on my temple and into my eyebrow that carried a texture I always had to wear bangs to cover.

I was introduced to One Drop Wonder™ by LimeLight in 2015, and started using it on these longstanding scars. Anyone who has ever dealt with scarring knows how hard it is to mend. And the older the scars, the harder they are to erase. Not so with One Drop Wonder™, as it turns out, because after some weeks of application, my old scars started changing.

When I finally met Todd Johnson nine months after I started using this amazing Pomifera® Oil, I told him my old scars had changed—so much that one could barely tell they were there. When I showed him the difference even he was amazed.

Now I'm able to wear my hair back without having to worry about it at all, and where it was sensitive before I sometimes have to remember that the scar is on my left side. Since then, I have often shared the experience with others. But even as I did, it was hard to convince people I had a scar. So, I started keeping an old picture of me on my smart phone, and they're literally taken aback by the before and after that they see.

I have been able to share this experience with so many others, and I'm constantly impressed myself with the other stories I hear about what this single product can do. It's certainly a core product of my LimeLight business. My business is doing great, and this is one of my biggest referral products because it does so many things so well.

My daughter Hayla likes to joke when she says: "One Drop Wonder...It cures world hunger."

Well...not quite. But it does a lot of remarkable things for so many people. It's done a lot for me, and I'm glad to share it.

~ *Sioux City, Iowa*

JANA DEFRINO: LIMELIGHT™

My experience with One Drop Wonder™ is nothing short of miraculous, especially due to the fact that it alleviated a problem I had been suffering with for nearly 10 years, and it started in the strangest way.

All my life, up through the age of 28, I had enjoyed perfect skin—and I mean not even a teenage run of acne—nothing. Then, all of a sudden at the age of 28, I broke out with what looked like I a skin allergy or something. It was diagnosed as rosacea but had an accompanying acne, which contradicted the analysis. So I had two or three things going on that just flared-up in my face and wouldn't go away.

It was unsightly. It was painful. And no one could seem to tell me what was wrong. Believe me, I tried everything to get rid of the problem. After a year or two I had been to, God knows, how many dermatologist—three or four at least.

I tried oral antibiotics, all of which failed miserably. (One even caused joint pain in my hips.) I tried steroids, which were terrible. I had cortisone shots in my face, which turned out to be a disaster.

I tried every topical cream and ointment. Nothing worked. No doctor ever helped me. No one was able to diagnose my condition correctly. I was in a constant state of disfigurement and distress. And my confidence as a wife and mother was shot.

By the time I'd joined LimeLight in 2015, I had run out of options. That's when I came across this new product called One Drop Wonder™, and this fascinating scientist named Todd Johnson who had just perfected this formula. And Oh, what a life-changing event that turned out to be!

When I finally learned about One Drop Wonder I had long since reached my wits end. So I thought, why not? What have I got to lose? I tried it according to Todd Johnson's guidelines, and after about two weeks of application I reached out to him to tell him that my condition had virtually cleared up. I wanted to put up my before and after photos—the end result was that conclusive. As far as I'm concerned this man is a genius, and this product is phenomenal.

Now I'm what they call a Founding Beauty Guide with LimeLight and I'm determined to share this experience. I know so many women and men have skin issues, and this product is out there to share. I'm determined to share this as often as I can, knowing it will help others when I do.

~Upper Saddle River, New Jersey

CHAPTER 11

FINDING THE LIMELIGHT

"Try not to become a man of success.
Rather, become a man of value."

~ Albert Einstein

At this point, there are two things about Pomifera® Oil that I find absolutely unique. First, it is the only element in Nature that is called an apple (hedge apple) and an orange (Osage orange). So that in itself creates a paradox. The other thing that amazes me to this day is the voicemail you get when you try to reach Todd Johnson on his cell phone. And it goes something like this:

"Hello, this is Todd Johnson of Pomifera. If you're calling about selling us hedge apples, I'm sorry we've reached our 1,000-ton limit for 2017. But please try us again in the fall of 2018. For all other calls please leave your number and I will get back in touch with you as soon as I can…"

Every time I hear it, I am at least somewhat amazed because this is a message no one would have put on their outgoing message box as recently as three years ago. Even today it is still a voicemail that is unique anywhere in the world, because Osage Healthcare, Inc. is still a company like no other.

That has to create a rush of some kind, especially if you're the guy who started it all. (Someone once referred to it as a "founder's rush" and that seems to be spot on.) I query Todd Johnson about both these issues before our upcoming Q & A, and he admits that it's still kind of fun to think about.

RJA: *A thousand ton limit! You've "reached your 1000 ton limit." That's quite a stockpile of hedge apples.*

Todd: And we may have to double that next year to meet demand. I'll just have to make that determination when we get there.

RJA: *Still...that almost seems like an arbitrary number. How did you arrive at that sum?*

Todd: Well, remember what it reduces down to. We have to spend a good bit of time and energy to extract a handful of seeds from all that lot, and then reduce and refine the oil from that. And yet that's what we do. So the actual numbers of hedge apples processed to extract a given amount of seeds and seed oil comes down to being pretty precise about the pile you buy.

RJA: *And you're making all these calculations and producing all this product based on new market demand.*

Todd: Which has jumped up by a quantum leap since last year.

RJA: *OK, now we're more or less bringing you up to date, because we're covering this last year and its upward arc from LimeLight*

Palooza in Orlando in 2016 and now (late in 2017). What kind of run has it been for you, and how did you get to this point? I mean you've really kicked your game to the next level.

Todd: Well, it is a kind of a cool thing to think about when I find the time. The bad news is that I really don't have much time to think about it these days, because we are so busy I almost have to stay on autopilot. Then again, that's the good news as well. Because I'm exactly where I hoped we'd be in five years. But what's the saying: "The toughest part of achieving real success is learning how to deal with it?"

I guess that's where we are. And yes! The toughest part right now is meeting the demand for product, which has spiked exponentially the last 18 months! Exponential growth for 18 months! Just let that wash over you for a moment. THANK YOU Limelight!

RJA: *OK. You're here now. But let's backtrack about a year and a half to that place just after the 2016 Palooza when you realized you were on the threshold of a breakthrough. And you were just being made aware of the sudden "celebrity status" you were being brought into with LimeLight. How did that make you feel?*

Todd: No doubt about it. Being loved and applauded gives you a tremendous feeling of accomplishment. I also realized that it's just human nature to confuse the messenger with the message. Sure, they liked me. Some might even be in awe of me (for whatever reasons). But what all these highly intelligent, career motivated women really wanted was access to more information and all the ways they could be empowered to be more effective in telling the story—the One Drop Wonder™ story.

Of course, I wanted to be more accessible to all these very bright professionals. But what I needed was a way to be available to them 24/7 in ways that could help them without entirely wiping out my personal business timetables. So, I had to seek the Social Media solution. I had to get Facebook friendly.

RJA: *And by your own admission, this was not your strong suit. But I'm guessing that you had two smart tech-savvy millennial daughters that did. And you probably went there for help.*

Todd: And you would be entirely correct. Almost as soon as I got back from Palooza 2016, I sent out an S.O.S. to Emily and Leah to come help me set up this whole Facebook and Twitter thing, and before too long I had a genuine social media presence, including about 3000 plus Facebook friends (and hundreds of followers). And you'd better believe that most of those are Lime-Light *Beauty Guides*.

RJA: *So, how long did it take to get you there? And what happened next?*

Todd: Well, like all things you do on social media, it blew up pretty quickly. Particularly coming in off the momentum of Palooza 2016 I had a ready, willing and able information-hungry audience.

What I had to do next was learn how to make the most of it. And from the beginning this was never about "me." Despite my being a pretty crowd-friendly speaker, I'm also a private person when it comes to family and to my personal need to restore, and recharge my batteries. I also understand that, with success, comes a responsibility to others.

So, in more ways than one, I was doing this by popular request because I knew it would help others grow. They could grow in their business and, I would hope, grow personally as well. For me, all of this was consistent with how I run Pomifera, I wanted to enable everyone to go out and represent One Drop Wonder™ in the most efficient and effective way possible.

Actually one of the first things we had to do after August of 2016 was get a more respectable online presence. So we completely updated our website, introduced a more complete representation of our product line, and created more of a specific identity.

Yes, to be sure, most of our key product was being represented by LimeLight in the form of One Drop Wonder™. But we certainly had to put on a prettier face to the rest of the world and to represent ourselves to that other segment of the market where we were still marketing hair and skin care products through a network of beauty schools, independent stylists and salons.

RJA: *Well, that seems like a given. But I guess there are times when image does have to catch up with reality. Is that what happened here?*

Todd: I think so. The good news is that our low profile might have made us unintentionally more mysterious. But once the lid is off the box, you have to step up and deliver. And one thing my personal page on Facebook has done for example is to create a kind of interactive forum for Beauty Guides and One Drop Wonder™ enthusiasts to come to me directly with questions about the product, requests for certain applications and even ideas and feedback for new products.

Now, I frequently go on my Facebook page and give regular updates (kind of like an online editorial) and make digital announcements of something new and exciting that's going on at Pomifera. Occasionally I'm able to conduct focus groups and feedback forums for new concepts. And my page has now become something of a headquarters for a number of product success stories and testimonials.

I'm amazed by the daily reports I get on how it is helping women and children of all ages—with skin problems, skin pathologies and allergies. And almost without exception, they are reporting phenomenal results. Some are even life changing experiences.

(I realize that sounds like I'm overselling it. But that is what is being reported back to me. So there's a special kind of reinforcement that comes with it.)

None of this is solicited, mind you. And we make no claims in these areas. Still, the feedback has been exceptional across the board. And we're able to chronicle a great many of those without agenda. They just show up on my timeline. I'm tagged on the stories. And they come from the heart.

RJA: *So this is kind of your online University of Pomifera. You're able to get everybody to tune you in, and so it's almost like a social media chat room.*

Todd: I think you were closer the first time. I'm actually able to go on my Facebook page and give instructional narrowcasts on its use and share any new findings I might have, as well as the usual exchange and feedback. I am primarily in education mode when I go online and talk about One Drop Wonder™.

RJA: *And what about new products? Do you use it to test the water on those?*

Todd: Well, yes and no! We reach out to LimeLight management first to gauge if they have any interest. And of course when you have something truly exciting and revolutionary—a hot new product—you want a trusted partner to have first option on distribution. That's where the big marketing muscle originates. And that's where it should always stay. Of course, their product packaging and presentation are absolutely stellar. So I know if LimeLight takes one of our products we are being put in the best possible light with a trusted high-preforming team for everyone from corporate department heads all the way down to a Beauty Guide in training. It's the best of both worlds.

RJA: *So, you've had tremendous results with the One Drop Wonder^TM, and it (and you) have become something of a legend.*

Todd: Well, sort of… the product maybe.

RJA: *And now you have come out with these Pomifera Bath Bombs. And they are apparently blowing up in their own right. Aren't they kind of the new superstars in LimeLight's panoply of personal care products?*

Todd: Yeah, they're officially called Pom Bombs™. And they really took off in ways I never expected. At this point, I've given up trying to predict the trends in personal care—what goes viral and what does not. All I know for now is that the Pom Bombs have become one of LimeLight's most popular products. It features no less than 15 drops of One Drop Wonder™, and it is so far ahead of the curve on this kind of product…who doesn't want to bathe in Pomifera® Oil?

RJA: *I was going to say, bath bombs have been around for about five years at least. So they're really nothing new. I know they're the market rage with Millennials, which is doubtless why your daughter Leah hit you up with the concept.*

Todd: …which I loved and no one else did. And the reason I knew this would work was because I did some evaluation of other bath bombs put out by the competition. Some of them were very popular products and yet their ingredients were mostly garbage. There were so many chemicals in most of them that people would be better off taking a dip in cheap shampoo and low grade oils. Well, maybe that's a bit of an exaggeration (but only a bit). The good news is that I knew we could come up with a Pomifera® Oil-based product that would knock their socks off. We have. It's lavish. And some of the feedback we've been getting is off the charts.

RJA: *And currently backordered…*

Todd: Which will change within the next week or two and certainly the time this book comes out. And by this time, we've learned to ramp up accordingly, and provide for additional inventory, even though we're not in the inventory business. Up to now, we have provided product in direct proportion to availability of packaging.

RJA: *"The only constant is Change." So what else has changed for you with Osage Healthcare Inc. and Pomifera Oil just since the beginning of 2017?*

Todd: Other than the usual growing pains and working 60-hour weeks, our relationship with LimeLight has deepened. They are now our exclusive distributor of Pom Bomb™ and One Drop Wonder™. And their distributor force has blown up to about three times its previous numbers in just a year.

I think "exponential growth" is the most consistent description that jumps to mind. Just from the demand for product, you can feel the pulse of this kind of group immediately. And that was most recently illustrated at the 2017 LimeLight Palooza in Austin.

RJA: *You were impressed and inspired by the reception you received in Orlando in 2016. What was the big difference in 2017's August gathering in Texas?*

Todd: The numbers, for one thing, were astounding. We had about 400 attendees in 2016. I nice sized crowd certainly, given the fact that the company was still on the ground floor and just starting to take off in a major way.

In 2017 the number of attendees had jumped to nearly 2,300. And it was almost overwhelming, because this time I really was more or less the "man of the hour." And I was truly being granted celebrity status whether I wanted it or not. I might add that being the "man of the hour" is easy when 95%+ of the attendees are women.

Believe me: I am completely out of my element in this kind of environment, because people approach you in ways that are not always entirely realistic and for reasons that have very little to do with you.

They're either shy and withdrawn around you because they look upon you as some sort of superstar. Or else they want to spend a lot of personal time with you and do a brain download, when this is not the kind of event that even remotely allows you to do that.

It's O.K. because I truly love the attention. The environment and positivity are absolutely intoxicating. And was great returning to this event to see how much LimeLight has grown during the previous twelve months. The energy was electric. The Beauty Guides were absolutely in great form and incredibly motivated. And the difference between stepping up in front of a room of 400 people and 2,300 people is all the difference in the world.

In really large gatherings, you get a kind of "stadium" environment. And the crowd becomes a creature all its own. You can actually feel the difference. There is a hunger for information and it's palpable.

Of course, here I am this "science guy" with a PhD in Chemistry and a lot of good ideas. (At least I hope they are.) So I get up in front of a crowd of women this size and the applause is deafening. And I get to see this and realize that this is something for which I can claim at least some responsibility for it all coming together. Still at the end of the day, I have never sold a single bottle of One Drop Wonder™. Only a LimeLight Beauty Guide can do that, so I give all of them the credit.

RJA: *I think that would be accurate. So what had changed and what were the constants you were able to enjoy? Or did you even get the chance?*

Todd: The best thing about much of it was seeing some old friends there and catching up with them…and learning how much the last year had meant for them and what contributions our products had made to their whole way of life. It was also quite a mob scene, and yes I was the focus of a great deal of attention.

Fortuitously I brought Susan along with me for this trip, so she could witness firsthand the kind of mob scene it was becoming. She had signed up as a LimeLight Beauty Guide (with Kendra Aarhus) the year before, plus being my strong "lieutenant" at Pomifera. So she was certainly here for all the right reasons. But I think even she was surprised at the energy level that transpired.

RJA: *Well, Susan is a very strong and accomplished woman. So I'm sure she took it all in stride? Or…was it stressful?*

Todd: Well, Susan and I have a very solid relationship on all levels. So yes! She took it all in stride. (And she had been warned… by me.) She ultimately reached a saturation point after a day or so, and I remember on the second day when she went up to the room to get a good night's sleep.

I decided to go down and get a bite to eat, and distinctly recall so many women in the hotel lobby that, when I wanted to get from the elevator to the bar, I only managed about 10 feet an hour.

And I actually get it. There is so much vibrancy in the room that you almost reach a point where it's an out-of-body experience. You're talking, sharing and interacting, and it goes on nonstop in a sort of chain reaction. At the same time you feel like you're watching yourself on television. It creates a level of detachment that is almost necessary.

231

Then again, it's also terrific to be in that position because you also have that feeling of a "family reunion." Some longtime relationships deepen and then they bring into your circle of experience a new energy as well. It's all very life affirming…even if it does take a while to get to the dinner table.

RJA: *Did you finally get to eat?*

Todd: Yes I believe I did. Right before the kitchen closed.

RJA: *OK. So, I guess the Austin Palooza was both good and challenging for all the right reasons. You've got to know it's only going to get bigger next time. Am I right?*

Todd: I think you are. In fact, we heard from LimeLight corporate that in 2018 they're expecting between 8,000 and 10,000 Beauty Guides to show up. That's a real game change.

RJA: *So how does that make you feel?*

Todd: I can only feel optimistic, hopeful and very bullish. I mean, at this point the sky is the limit. And it's already reached that level of popularity that is far beyond what I had expected it to be at this point.

Even more than that…this is the fifth year in our capital payback plan for Osage Healthcare, Inc. to be completely financially solvent. And we are already closing-in on some considerable liquidity.

RJA: *I know you've got some major product line expansions coming up for 2018.*

Todd: We are branching out in so many areas—with new products, with new clients, with the expansion of One Drop Wonder™ into Europe (and globally). So we now literally have the opportunity to become a global brand.

Because of LimeLight's new partner agreement with L'Occitane, a giant personal care company out of France, we are expanding Pomifera® Oil (as One Drop Wonder™) into a major product proliferation in European Markets.

Right now, we're just sticking our toe in the water with them. But L'Occitane has a superb track record when it comes to launching new products with attainable sales goals in mind. So there is no telling where One Drop Wonder™ can go with the kind of aggressive marketing and product positioning this group does.

RJA: *I've heard of L'Occitane (de Provence). They are one of the most influential personal care companies no one has heard about. (At least not in America.) I do know this much about them: They are very quick to develop and market new products they find worthy of the brand. Is this where they are with you?*

Todd: Yes! It's headed that way. Apparently, when LimeLight management introduced the product line to L'Occitane for possible affiliations, they were very taken with One Drop Wonder™. So far, we seem to be pushing at an open door wherever we go.

RJA: *And you are still developing and formulating new products for LimeLight?*

Todd: Not surprisingly, the Pom Bombs™ are taking off so well that we're designing and developing theme formulations in different aromas and treatment combinations in an effort to offer holiday and seasonal bath bombs though LimeLight during 2018.

They're various presentations of the same product, and yet they are something completely different. It's definitely the kind of spinoff that people have been requesting. So I know there is a built-in acceptance for them going in.

RJA: *And you have some developmental formulations you're working on in the areas of healing in both skin care focused on face, bath and body products.*

Todd: My lips are sealed. But yes we are, and we're excited about that as well. Right now everything we seem to be doing is unfolding a new avenue of demand. So, by now, Pomifera® Oil's reputation is spawning a new rush of potential clients.

The way it stands now, I have, in a non-binding way, extended a right of first refusal agreement with our friends at LimeLight. So they're always going to get the first bite at the apple…

RJA: *Just had to say that, didn't you?*

Todd: Couldn't resist. Anyway, they do in every sense of the word, before we consider other markets and other relationships for our technology. And of course, we still have that complete apron of potential with the proprietary aspects of this amazing oil, which I am (at some point) honor bound to research and develop, later if not sooner.

RJA: *OK. So here you are—where you want to be. (At least I assume you are.) What would you like right now that you don't have?*

Todd: A little more time to catch up. Right now, we are just scrambling to fulfill product orders. And it's definitely part of the plan only to expand when the market volume absolutely demands it. That way, you have no choice to do otherwise.

So, yes! I would like to take a breather. And yes! I'm thrilled to death to be working my buns off with my staff and just enjoying the fruits of our labor.

RJA: *And you're getting more visible, which I guess means you have to be more accessible online. Is that still an issue?*

Todd: No. Because I only do it when I want to or need to. And I've come to accept Alexander Graham Bell's maxim that "for every increase in technology there will be a proportionate loss of privacy."

After all, at this point, we all live in a fish bowl. So you may as well enjoy trying to become a Big Fish.

RJA: *And you're a big presence on Facebook. What about Twitter? Have you ever figured that out?*

Todd: No.

RJA: *Neither have I.*

Todd: Must work for some people. In fact it already has.

RJA: *Could get you elected President.*

Todd: Not running any time soon.

RJA: *So what is your next goal? To continue to become that "Big Fish?" Do you want to continue this level of success?*

Todd: Well, it's all pretty relative. Everyone wants to continue to succeed. More important, I think, is the innate need to "achieve" that needs to be what your end game should be. I say that because perceptions of success and all the popularity that goes along with it can end up being an illusion. The reality is in getting to achieve the next big thing—make the next discovery—the one that will change lives.

I think it was Einstein who said, "Try not to be a man of success. Rather become a man of value."

I think anyone in my field knows the difference. And therein lies the key.

CHAPTER 12

"A PERFECT WORLD"

"There is no such thing as perfection.
But on the way to seeking it, we may achieve excellence."

~ Vince Lombardi

The final thing I've learned in this process is that Todd Johnson understands Milestones and the importance of honoring them. It is not ego that drives him to do this but a sense of legacy. And that is an awareness of one's role in life that very few men come to grips with; until it's too late.

Todd isn't one to wait around. This whole book, in its way, has been a gamble and his unique way of leaping ahead of convention. Pioneers do that.

At the moment, Todd is surviving the Christmas/New Year's holiday recovering from a mild stomach virus, embracing a bushel basket of gratitude and facing "Twin Peaks"—mounds of hedge apples and product orders (one being promptly refined to fulfill the other).

Right now it's approaching another Polar Vortex in the Midwest. Temperatures are dropping below zero, and everything will harden up and become more difficult to negotiate. Space heaters will have to come out, and the processing will get sticky and slower for a while. (It is a temperature thing.)

Todd looks around his mini-stronghold in his 3,500 square foot facility and realizes, in a very good way, that he has at last maxed out.

"This is all going to need an upgrade and shortly," he observes with a readable sense of nostalgia for what will soon become an appendage at best to an entire new level of development.

I join him in that reminiscence, as he turns to me, this time initiating the Q & A.

Hello, this is Todd Johnson of Pomifera. If you're calling about selling us hedge apples, I'm sorry we've reached our 1000-ton limit..."

Todd: We rent this whole setup – office and warehouse and processing facility for $1250 a month. And at this point, it has generated over several million dollars in revenue. Not a bad return on investment. It also aligns with my saying: Low on thrills, high on margin, take care of your employees.

RJA: *A bit of an oversimplification I suppose. There are a lot of factors that go into this beyond the brick and mortar and the four walls. But I get the metaphor. Did you think it would happen this fast and to this degree?*

Todd: When you're dealing with what amounts to the best possible combination of revolutionary natural product based technology that combines to form a unique product, it becomes lightning in a bottle. Whatever you use to contain it is probably not going to be enough.

That's a very good thing, and yet disconcerting in a way, because it's a lot like downhill racing for a skier. You push the envelope just enough to still be in control, knowing all the while that you may crossover into that danger zone where everything is coming at you and all you can do is react, rely on your instincts and trust in the process.

RJA: *So that's where you are now?*

Todd: Yes, we're going to have to expand and modernize in every area. The issue now is one of prioritization. We have the brand of Pomifera®. We own it. And we are at least three seasons ahead of anyone with a similar inclination before the competition can even think of something.

There are very few companies with a signature product—one that at this point cannot be easily duplicated. Add to that the fact that I was able to pluck this gem out of Nature as a completely unexpected organic entity, with its own category shelf in God's Pharmacy, and that's a pretty special feeling.

But at this point, it goes beyond that. Because what touches me most is that we have constructed a whole new level of synergy—plus a new community that didn't exist before.

RJA: *And a new industry.*

Todd: It gives one a sense of real pioneering. We have broken new ground in a very literal sense in so many areas. And that feels terrific. What feels better is the sense of coming home to Iowa, building something in Iowa and based upon an abundant natural resource relevant to Iowa.

RJA: *We'll you are the Johnny Appleseed of Pomifera. Maybe they'll build a monument in your honor in Des Moines or something!*

Todd: Ha ha! A bit of a stretch! But what it does for me is remind me, in no uncertain terms, that with my chosen field—Chemistry—all things are possible. It is a field virtually without limits and it crosses over into life in so many ways. There are elements, complete in themselves, and yet seemingly infinite in their permutations. The potentials for combination, once expanded, become endless.

RJA: *Speaking of "endless…" you've got a lot of ramping up to do in the next year or so. Do you even know where you're going to begin?*

Todd: Yes, it's really pretty exciting to realize that about a year from now all of this will be changed and a whole new dynamic will be taking its place. We'll certainly have to begin with production, expand output, and hire more people, easily double the staff we have now.

Given our current rate of growth, we may double or even triple staff within the next 9-18 months. There is no way of telling for certain.

I've always had as my heroes and role models the people that we most often refer to as "Futurists." They are the visionaries—the Howard Roarks, Marie Curies and Nikola Teslas of the world.

They see years or even decades ahead. They plan strategically. But what is also needed to match those strategies is to be able to follow through logistically.

RJA: *Are you going to be able to do that?*

Todd: I thought you were going to stop asking rhetorical questions. *[He winks.]* Then again, I suppose it is a legitimate concern because this is where most people trip up.

To answer that query, absolutely yes! In addition to Osage Healthcare, Inc. purchasing our current building and 12 acres of land, Susan I have personally purchased 40 more acres of land locally, with plans to grow non-GMO oil producing crops to vertically integrate wherever we determine that's the best way to do it.

Once you get used to having skin the game, as we have by now, you have to make a lot of smart decisions. You have to think on your feet. You still have to take risks. By all measures we should take more risk rather than less. By this time most of my judgment is informed by experience. So my instincts are highly tuned and I've learned to trust them.

And I've learned to trust my people—all of them. In purely operational terms, we are completely interchangeable. If anything goes wrong for a moment or even a day, there is always the "next person up."

RJA: *That sounds awfully good. But do you really mean it? When you get right down to it, is Todd Johnson irreplaceable?*

Todd: I certainly hope so. Operationally I am being replaced. As the scientific expert, inventor of new products, and face of Pomifera® that may be a bit difficult to back fill. My training at Monsanto and the systems I helped set up at places like ABC and Cambrex drive to that model. It's something I believe in absolutely. (A chain is only as strong as its weakest link.) And in the logical scheme of things, we are all eventually going to be replaced. Duplication is a natural progression. And life and death are just God's way of telling us he has a job for us someplace else.

RJA: *But right here, right now, you've got a lot more you want to accomplish just with Pomifera right?*

Todd: Oh, without question. I think we're just scratching the surface of what Pomifera® Oil might be able to do. And it does so without any significant rate of decomposition, it has very low rates of allergic reaction, and seems to be endless in its beneficial applications to skin. And one I've been blessed enough to tap into. Truly better to be lucky than good.

RJA: *OK. Let's take this scenario five to ten years down the road to its inevitable happy ending. You have potentially maxed out your Pomifera empire (or certainly reached the summit), and at this point there are no worlds left to conquer. Are you going to be planning your retirement? Or are you going to continue churning and burning on new projects? Is there another Pomifera out there waiting to be discovered?*

Todd: Those are a lot of questions. So let me take them in reverse order. First, I've already noted the hundreds of thousands of plant species in the world. And among those 5,200 are for food and more than 15,000 are medicinal. Half of those have yet to be tapped into, either because of their incredible complexity or because they're geographically inaccessible.

Then we get into what is possible and even available. I'm betting there are two dozen or so very potent, valuable, overlooked species within about 500 miles of Bloomfield, Iowa at this very moment. And maybe half of those are some abandoned Native American pharmacopeia just waiting for some "mad scientist" like me to come along and bring it back into the light. Reveal their destiny so to speak.

Last but by no means least, I will never abandoned the Pomifera® brand, partners, and opportunity for innovative natural product development until they absolutely can be abandoned or they abandon me. Always leave things better than you found them....

RJA: *So that would be a "yes." You would take on another Pomifera challenge in your life.*

Todd: I am, at my core, a chemistry nerd. I love picking up small pieces of the universe and asking "is there something interesting in there?" There's so much unknown... and such infinite potential. Getting a glimpse of how something works gives one an immediate sense of immortality. It is still the undiscovered universe, and I have passage. I say that in all gratitude. I'm sure you know that.

RJA: *Speaking of gratitude, are you happy with where you are at this point?*

Todd: Pretty much.

RJA: *And what are you most grateful for?*

Todd: The women in my life. My daughters Leah and Emily, and my beautiful wife, Susan. I'm so proud of them all. And they're my partners, teachers and inspirations every single day...and, of course, the rest of my family. We haven't spoken much about my mother, but I want everyone to know that she was the first woman to have a positive influence on me. I have a great family and wonderful friends. I'm a lucky man.

RJA: *What do you think is your best quality?*

Todd: Well… maybe I have two or three that kind of weigh in equally for me.

The first is my ability to forgive and forget. I never hold grudges, because they just bind you even more closely to the object of your resentment. So I have always had an ability to just put things behind me and absolutely get them out of my mind. I don't believe in holding on. I'd rather keep moving on.

And that kind of ties into another quality I rely on, and that is my inner drive. I just keep pressing forward. I never look back, and I never want to let down. The thought of backsliding or giving up really bothers me. If you're not moving forward, you're not progressing, and I always want to be out there finding a situation and making something better out of it.

The last thing I guess I like about myself is my utter lack of unnecessary greed. I'm just not hard-wired to be that greedy. I think that can be self-destructive. I want to be able to treat people well rather than trying to squeeze an extra buck out of them. Don't get me wrong. I like abundance. And once you've been poor you become absolutely driven never to be poor again. I always want to able to provide for my family and make sure that I can generate a secure work environment at Pomifera®.

RJA: *Well, I think you've done that rather successfully. You have one daughter who's a successful RN/BSN, and another in a pre-veterinary program at Iowa State. Both are kind, honest, enlightened women that know how to balance drive and success in a graceful manner. Your wife Susan is your partner in the business. So, deal sealed! What is your greatest weakness, do you think?*

Inventor Mike Bailey with Todd Johnson.

Todd: Hmmm… probably my inability to just kickback and take some time off for myself. I need to create more downtime. But I never seem to get around to it.

RJA: *Would you even if you could? I mean, you strike me as one of the most driven men I've ever met. And you actually seem to enjoy every minute of it.*

Todd: Ah! But am I driven? Or am I being "guided?" The latter question suggests that I really should live and project with a bit more humility as I lean forward into the universe.

RJA: *Is that a rhetorical question? Maybe that's a good way to end the book.*

Todd: Well, the book ends, but the story continues. That's the beauty of technology. From what you've told me, with electronic books, you can always add new chapters. So let's not call this an ending. Let's just call this "Phase One."

Footnote: Almost organically, Todd completes his conversation with me in a way that tells me there will always be "more." As in a journey that one has enjoyed taking, there is so much to record—always something left unsaid, and questions you wish you had asked.

But like all relationships with visionaries, there remains that crack in the door, left ajar and open to let in the light.

POMIFERA*oil*™

WHERE FOLKLORE MEETS BEAUTY™

ACKNOWLEDGMENTS

Acknowledgements are about gratitude. The Author would like to thank so many people who helped contribute to the inspiration, creation and content of this book. They include (in no special order), his Great Uncle Don Prevo (for his guidance and inspiration) his father Doy Johnson for always being his rock, good friend Stan Huggins, his professor/mentors Drs. Lou Messerle, Ken Caulton and John Gladyz, and his many brilliant working associates, including Mike Stern, Gary Mossman, Eric Neuffer, Dennis Riley, Joe Nettleton, Steve Klosk, Travis Mickle, and especially his longtime friend and business partner Erik Tjaden. He would further like to extend both his appreciation to and admiration for Michele Gay and Madison Mallardi of Lime-Light, Kendra Aarhus for her loyalty and Advocacy and for all the LimeLight family of "beauty guides" who have shown their support and contributions to this book. Included among them are Jana DeFrino, Erin Jean Doohen and Natasha Ramsey, as well as so many others. He would also like to thank his publisher Fideli Publishing, his co-author Robert Joseph Ahola and all those who have taken the time to read, review and praise this work of the heart. Above all else, Todd would like to thank the rest of his wonderful family—his mother Mary Ellen, his brother Mike, sister Vicki and his wonderful wife and life mate Susan, as well as his daughters Emily and Leah who make this wonderful journey of life worth taking.

ABOUT THE AUTHORS

Todd Johnson has led a blessed life. Having risen out of the trailer courts of Southern Iowa to the boardrooms of corporate America, Todd has buttressed his Chemistry Ph.D. with common sense to bring to life a healing seed oil called Pomifera® Oil. Todd is the holder of dozens of peer reviewed scientific articles and patents. He has recently transitioned from drug development to an Eastern medicinal approach to healing skin. A self-confessed nerd, he now spends his time living in the world of beauty as the founder of the Pomifera® Oil revolution—Where Folklore Meets Beauty. ☺

Robert Joseph Ahola is an author, playwright, and producer in Malibu, California with over 50 awards for excellence. He is an author/co-author of fourteen published books including *The Return of the Hummingbird Wizard, I, Dragon,* and *Africa Arrives.* He has authored twelve published plays, including Judas Agonistes, *NARCISSUS/The Last Days of Lord Byron, Pavlov's Cats* and *The Decline and Fall of Us All.* He has scripted six screenplays including *Whitman, The Attack of the Robot Bees* and the upcoming TV Series: *Master of Discretion. THE HEDGE,* written with Todd Johnson, is his fourth biography.

www.ingramcontent.com/pod-product-compliance
Lightning Source LLC
Chambersburg PA
CBHW051243020426
42333CB00025B/3036